Suitcase Full of Dreams

"This well-written book starts with Hoy Kersh sharing her first memory of fear as her family whisks her off to another state, running for their lives from Klan members who have sworn to kill them. Ms. Kersh then tells the story of her early life: anecdotes about friends and family, the prejudices she faced, and the events that shaped her beliefs. This is a woman who lived through a tumultuous period in our nation's history, and put her painful childhood memories on paper for the world. Her book should be required reading for high school and college students."

— Luann Morgan, *Reading Frenzy*

"I would have loved to have had a copy of **Suitcase Full of Dreams** to use as a teaching resource. While we studied Toni Morrison, Alice Walker, Maya Angelou, John Steinbeck, Anne Frank's diary, and various contemporary and classic women writers, Hoy's story would have added dimension and raw truth to the enduring issues and themes these other great writers explored. I was moved to tears and to laughter by this book. Hoy's clear voice and conversational style speaks to me of poverty, oppression, racism, religion, the transformative powers of education, and most of all, love. Her language is poetic; she paints beautiful, detailed pictures with her words, and brings to life engaging characters and experiences that haunt me even now."

— Denise Lowe Thorngate, teacher of English and Drama

Suitcase Full
of Dreams

"*After reading* **Suitcase Full of Dreams**, *I found myself at a loss for words, unable to describe the emotions—joy, anger, frustration, loss, and loving care—that were moving through me. I read Hoy's life story late into the night and in stolen moments throughout the day, and have emerged with an understanding that I would not have thought possible. This is an important and moving read on many levels.*"
— Stephen Quiggle, M.A., Counseling Psychologist

"**Suitcase Full of Dreams** *is an interesting and entertaining memoir. In her unique writing style, Hoy Kersh tells of a life of poverty, abuse at home, segregation, and killings by the KKK. Anyone who wants to know what life was like for poor blacks in the South before the Civil Rights Movement will enjoy reading this memoir.*"
— *Different Time, Different Place Book Reviews*

Suitcase Full of Dreams

Hoy Kersh

Cozilove
ENTERPRISES

Suitcase Full of Dreams
© 2010 Hoy Kersh

Hoy Kersh
Cozilove Enterprises
PO Box 514
Whitethorn, CA 95589

Book design by Cypress House
Cover design by John Angus

Special thanks to my editors—
Michael Denneny and Denice Wedderford.

"Strange Fruit"
By Lewis Allan
Copyright © 1939 (Renewed) by Music Sales Corporation
International Copyright Secured. All Rights Reserved.
Used by Permission.

Library of Congress Control Number: 2009935580

Printed in the USA
2 4 6 8 9 7 5 3 1

First edition

Mixed Sources
Product group from well-managed
forests and other controlled sources
www.fsc.org Cert no. SW-COC-002283
© 1996 Forest Stewardship Council
FSC

To Rotary Rob —
one love in our
ble*ssed* community.

This book is dedicated
to the vision of
world peace.

one love, Hey

Chapter 1

A Child is Born and the Heavens Sing

I left the South so long ago, never to return, never looking back to allow yesterday to flood on in. Most likely the images from my past will disturb me, break through the barriers guarding my heart. Maybe blame it on the softness of the day, the sweet smell of the earth after the morning rain, the sun so hot it burns through me; whatever the reason, I surrender and see her, see me. A brown-eyed little girl tugs gently on my hand. Seems like she calls me from a distant shore. I answer her and the past floods into the present, Mississippi, Alabama, Grandma Emma, Mama, and Daddy. The life I walked away from, buried deep inside my chest, has come to life again, and the tears stream softly. Laughter, sorrow, good times, hard times all exposed.

My faded birth certificate reveals so little. Yet I have it until this day. Mother's name, Mabel Elease; colored; housekeeper, twenty-two years old. Father's name, James Cosmore; colored; painter, twenty-four years old. Mama's firstborn, Walter, died at six months, and Bobby was three when I was born on January 24, 1941, in Clarksdale, Mississippi. Cohoma County; home of the blues, run-down shacks, and cotton fields. I was named Catherine Rose.

Mama named me after two white women she worked for. Gentle, middle-aged spinsters who loved her and treated her with respect. Miss Catherine was thin as a stick. Her eyes were almost violet colored, with the laugh lines around her mouth that happy people get. She was a teacher at the big white high school on St. Joseph's Avenue. That was the street we coloreds walked on only when we were going to work, the neighborhood where the well-to-do whites lived.

Miss Rose was dark, olive skinned. Her hair was so thick, straight, and black, Mama was sure she was part Indian. Her brown eyes were welcoming to strangers and friends alike. Mama worked at their big white house the whole time she was carrying me. Miss Rose was a librarian and made sure Mama had books to read. Mama had to work hard. Black men hardly ever made good money, so the women worked too.

These two ladies believed in blacks having the right to vote; and being allowed in integrated schools. Whites who had thoughts like that had to be careful back then. They would be considered nigger lovers, outcasts in their own community. Yep, those women loved us. Mama said they were born way ahead of their time.

They stayed in our lives, and never forgot Mama. She rode the bus to their house five days a week working long hours, cleaning, hand washing their clothes, and cooking their evening meal. She scrubbed from the front steps to the back porch on her hands and knees, pregnant and happy, with tired feet and a young woman's heart. Miss Catherine and Miss Rose bought my baby clothes, soft gauzy gowns, brand-new diapers, and a colorful baby quilt they made for me because they surely loved my Mama.

Mama had my brother Bobby and said she dreamed for a daughter. Mama said, "The Lord heard my prayers and sent you to us, Cat." I had a dresser drawer for my bed, and the green fertile deltas of Mississippi for my home. Mama, with her warm brown arms, kept me from the cold dark days of winter.

Every time Mama would tell me about my birth, I'd hold my breath. "Cat, it was a star-filled, cold January night when you decided to come. You were born with double pneumonia and couldn't catch your breath. The midwife, Miss Letitia, dunked you in cold water, then hot, till you gasped and life came on in. The sweet air filled your lungs and your little blue body became brown. We all rejoiced."

Grandma Emma's story was, "Cat, it sure seems like you were afraid to come to this earth, almost as if your eyes saw too far. I swear the angels were holding you back." Mama didn't like Grandma to contradict her facts, and it seemed to be Mama's habit to belittle Grandma. She quickly said, "Nonsense, Miss Emma, It was just pneumonia. You're filling her head with dreams." Grandma just smiled gently. I believed her. My grandma always spoke the truth to me.

I was born in good-old Clarksdale, Mississippi, south of Memphis, a raggedy little town, no dreams of future prosperity, just getting along. Abandoned plantations, resplendent in their decay, echo their long-gone owners' decadence. Cotton fields stretch as far as the eye can see. Miles of colored settlements full of run-down shacks start outside of town. Poor white farmers live apart from us, but we all lived on red clay roads. The ponds were full of catfish and bass. There was wild game to hunt and mules to haul crops. Poverty littered the streets like confetti. Confederate flags flew proudly in that Ku Klux Klan town.

Mississippi is the birthplace of the blues. The home of B. B. King, Howling Wolf, Louise Johnson, John Lee Hooker, Muddy Waters — the list unfurls like a rainbow ribbon on a clear blue windy day. Our music was rooted in this hot, cotton-growing, lush delta land whose soil was considered the finest on the earth.

Oh, sweet sorrows and soft tomorrows, where the river shines and there is always the promise that things will get better. Daddy said he had it made in that sleepy Mississippi town. His father was the German sheriff, and my grandma was his black mistress. Grandma said we lived well, in a white house with a wraparound porch where honeysuckle and night-blooming jasmine perfumed the air. Daddy always remembers the birds singing freely in our yard, as they will where trees and flowers are.

My daddy met Mama when she worked in a chicken shack in Clarksdale, Mississippi. My Mama was a beautiful, doe-eyed, young brown waitress. She was short, wasn't five feet tall, but comely as a spring flower; fragrant and newly blossomed. My Daddy was the town run-around. He wore new clothes, always had pocket money, and was well known. He was good-looking and knew it. Even though he worked as a janitor, he had money enough to woo Mama and convince her to marry him.

We were better off than most. Our house was large enough to hold us all. Daddy's father, Shorty he was called, didn't live with us. He openly supported Grandma and my daddy, but lived with his wife, Miss Barbara Ann, on the other side of the railroad tracks where the white people lay their heads to sleep. It was a guaranteed lynching for a black man to sleep with a white woman, but being as he was the sheriff, Grandpa openly took care of us. He owned the land and house we lived in, and loved us all.

I don't remember too much about my grandpa. His skin smelled like the cigarettes he smoked, along with the scent of warm sun and the peppermint candy he was always sucking on to keep his stomach happy. He walked with that certain swagger short men get. Grandma towered over him — she was six feet tall in her bare feet, and Grandpa was only five foot seven. Even though Grandpa was short, he talked loud enough to be heard way down the block and was not someone to ignore. He was a handsome man, judging from the few pictures we had of him. His brown eyes seemed to be looking far into the horizon. Grandpa's thick brown hair fell into his eyes, and he was always brushing it back under his hat. His face was slender and his mouth looked drawn, never smiling too much. I remember him riding us on his shoulders, laughing as if the world was ours, and it was for those moments we waited. But Grandpa looked stern when he wore his uniform and gun. His smile was not there then, and I never wanted to hug him too close.

We walked in a world where white people lived distant and very few smiled at us. More than once Grandpa would come over to our house looking like the whole world rode his shoulders. I'd run up and jump into his arms, and instead of hugging me tight he'd talk real quiet to Grandma. "Shorty," she'd almost whisper, "what's wrong?" He'd usually sit at the kitchen table while Grandma made his coffee, and quietly tell her of his day. Another black man killed, another white man killed. Grandpa said, "Emma, poverty and ignorance rule this land." His soul struggled in that Southern town.

Daddy told us how he wore the best of clothes, had credit everywhere, and lived the life of the privileged few. He and Grandma still had to work, and money didn't come easy, but Daddy was spoiled by Grandpa and never went without. He was still a black man, but his daddy being the sheriff definitely helped. Everything seemed to be good as it could be in that mean old town until the night Grandpa was shot to death.

Grandma Emma always thought the Klansmen killed him, as Grandpa had the habit of speaking the truth, voicing words of reason in the mighty land of hatred. Also, Grandpa might have been involved in some moonshine smuggling. He was shot in his chest and left to die alone in a lonely alley behind the local bar.

That night, as the new silver moon hung in the black summer sky, while Grandpa's soul was leaving his body and his blood bathed the damp ground, the Klansmen came to our house. There must have been thirty or forty men dressed in white robes. They were a sinister crowd. With hoods over their faces, they carried torches and shotguns. Surrounding the house, one of them called Grandma out to the front porch and told her, "Leave before morning, nigger woman." My Grandma was well known and respected, and my father was better off gone than hung.

The dark forces had their way and we were running for our lives. I was way too little to understand that night of terror, but the tale has been told so many times. I can see it, taste the fear, feel Grandma's heart beat way too fast, and see Mama's young woman face become old for the moment. Daddy was mostly in shock. His daddy gone, murdered, no time to visit his grave, no time to say goodbye. To try to visit his Daddy's grave would bring him death.

What a dark, terror-filled night that was. Three years old, and my world was changing. I remember clutching the rag doll Mama made me. My eyes were fixed on Grandma Emma's big frame so bent down, her face looking like wood, with tears streaming down her cheeks. I could only sit still as Mama insisted, and hold on to Bobby's hand as the grownups hurriedly packed Grandma's old Model T, one gift from Grandpa that saved our lives. The neighboring farmers brought us enough gas from their barns to get us to Mobile, as we did not dare stop. Mama's cedar chest held all she valued. They packed pots, pans, dishes, blankets, and clothes, all the things Grandma could fit into the car. We were loaded down. On that loveliest of spring nights, the woods fragrant and damp, my Dad was nervous. "Hurry, Hurry!" We drove out of Mississippi as quickly as that car could travel.

Aunt Sunny, Grandma's sister, was older than Grandma and was settled comfortably in Mobile, so we had a place to go. Her wide smile and dancing eyes welcomed us. Grandma loved Shorty; they weren't married but she was his for life. He openly loved her and my Daddy, but there was no time for tears, these were to flow quietly when Grandma was alone. When I asked Grandma if she missed my grandpa, she looked me dead in my young eyes and told me, "Cat, the stars over my head comfort me, the wind whispers in my ear, and the nightingale sings so sweet to let me know Shorty is here with me." We all need a warm bed, someplace safe to lay our heads, a little room to let in the light and the sweet fragrance of the green earth. When the day fades away, everybody needs someplace to stay.

Aunt Sunny, like my grandma, was tall as any man and had an attitude to boot. She was reddish brown, slim of waist and her eyes matched the midnight sky. Aunt Sunny would be called rakish if she were a man. Her hat was always pulled down over one eye and she most always had a feather of some kind sticking jauntily from her hatband, my kind of woman. Aunt Sunny was married to Uncle Rogers, who, unlike her, was shy. His quiet manners and short stature belied the greatness of his soul. Uncle Rogers was a carpenter and never lacked for work. He got Daddy his first job painting, and the two of them were a great pair, Uncle Rogers with his carpenter's apron on, and Daddy in his white paint clothes. Daddy always whistled when he worked, and came home every payday with treats for Mama and us.

Aunt Sunny worked the gypsum plant on the weekdays and gambled and partied the weekends. She would be laughing so loud because she won money, or just dancing for the joy of it. We kids loved to stay over at her house, sleeping on blankets on the floor. The house was tiny, painted blues and lavenders, with soft white curtains she sewed. Their home seemed like heaven to us, plus there were lots and lots of kids waiting to play. The red clay roads were quiet and dusty, great for walking barefoot. We girls spent hours dressing our dollies. We played baseball half the day, flew kites, and were just happy running and shrieking with laughter. The blue sky smiled down on us and the air was warm with the joy of being young and alive. The nights were meant for hide-and-go-seek, while the grownups sat on the front porches laughing at our antics.

We stayed a couple of weeks with Aunt Sunny and Uncle Rogers till Aunt Sunny found us some rooms to rent down the road from her, at Miss Lily's House.

We rented two rooms from Miss Lily and Mr. Harry, quiet Christian people who were raising their daughter's child, Denise. Her mama, like many others, had moved to Detroit to work and left her in the care of her grandparents. Mama said better people never walked the earth. They lived on a dusty road at the end of town, surrounded by the woods, so nature was our solace.

Miss Lily was tall, real quiet, and kind. Her eyes were green-brown and she smelled like the woods and the flowers in her garden. Mr. Harry was a railroad man, with rich chocolate skin, and a loud laugh. Denise, their granddaughter, was brown-eyed, and a good Christian girl. This meant no makeup, no red fingernails, no tight skirts with the sweater worn backwards, no attempt at all to look sexy, just clean and boring. Oh, brother. In comparison, we were so rotten, so bad, ready to cuss, have spitting contests, play cards, have farting contests, and belch loud — all the silly things kids love to do. Oh, no, not Denise. Naturally we were never too bad around her, plus she was fourteen and to her we were invisible.

Miss Lily and Mr. Harry owned their house, and the gardens were full. There were chickens, and big white geese who tormented us, chasing us with their huge wings furiously flapping. When they came at us, we had to run for our lives. They grew peaches, apples, fig trees, and blackberries in their field. We were lucky Grandma got to rent with us. Her little yellow, flower-surrounded room overlooked the back garden. She had a little verandah with a porch swing. Mobile, Alabama, welcome home.

Grandma loved to sit under the magnolia tree in the backyard, her chair under its branches. She would rock silently long after everyone had turned in for the evening. I would know she was out there because the night sky gave us both relief, me in seeing fairies and knights in the stars, and Grandma just probably seeing what grownups saw, couldn't know for sure. Her memories flowed like summer rain in the silent Alabama night.

My grandma was the pillar of our family, and she never let us hear her complain. Grandma was able to get on with life. She had her sister with her now, and she started laughing more. She was forty years old and still a good-looking woman. She'd put her hands on her wide hips and declare, "Life is good, darling."

Grandma owned that car and was smart. It didn't take her long to figure out that driving people back and forth to the doctor, to work, taking people shopping downtown, and picking up orders for stores always kept her in money, because hardly anyone owned a car. Her life quickly filled up with new friends. Miss Emma was well known in Mississippi, and Mobile was soon her new home.

Daddy missed his father. Some days he would curse and tell Grandma, "I'm going back to Clarksdale to see my daddy's grave. I can go and be back before anybody knows." Grandma seemed to always be reminding him, "J.C., you got a wife and two children who need you. Leave the past behind." Daddy was a man of few words, but his eyes would become scary when he was upset. His painting jobs kept him busy, and soon enough he had his buddies in the yard on the weekends, getting fishing gear together, or oiling their shotguns and rifles to hunt deer or wild pigs. Daddy was a good man who hated to kill anything and only hunted to feed us.

I could always tell when Mama missed her home, her girlfriends, Aunt Hattie and Uncle T.C., Miss Catherine, and Miss Rose. She would get that dewy, gray, before-the-rains-come look, and absently stroke her apron. Sometimes Mama would give one of her long sighs and start singing her favorite spiritual, "Swing Low, Sweet Chariot." Mama could paint the world with her voice. This song was enough to make us hear that railroad whistle in the night. That feeling of moving, leaving. The letters she got from Mississippi made her day and ours too. Mama's smile warmed even the coldest day.

Mama was twenty-seven years old. She was born in March, and nothing seemed to stop her. She was determined to make new friends, and her sewing circle was the winning ticket. Almost every Saturday afternoon, Mama, Miss Lily, Miss Dora, Miss Terrecina, and Miss Geraldine gathered at each other's houses to sew quilts, crochet, and embroider dresses. They enjoyed each other's gossip, iced tea, tuna sandwiches, laughter, and friendship. We loved it. The ladies brought their kids over, Kali, Charlotte, Tillie, and Portia. They sewed and we played. The days were gentle, our laughter sweetening the air like honey.

Kali was Miss Dora's youngest son, and he was her favorite. He was born sickly and had to stay home a lot. They lived next door to Miss Lily, and I was at home in their green shaded yard. Miss Dora would call me over the azalea hedge, "Cat, come on over now. Kali is feeling well today, and I just cut open a sweet watermelon." Miss Dora's eyes were light brown; they seemed to shine out golden lights from her dark brown face, and we loved her.

Kali's sister Tillie was eight. She would bring comic books over and try to read them to us: *Batman and Robin, Wonder Woman*, and *Little Lulu*. Whatever words she didn't know, it didn't matter, she would make them up. Tillie sometimes would act bossy and tell us, "Be quiet, sit still, stop giggling," and we would settle down. She had the power.

I swear changes have always scared the bejesus out of me. I have always wanted to hold moments of golden happiness close to my chest, cradled in my hands, security, soft rain, familiar roads, yep, that was Miss Lily's house to me. We loved her wide front porch, with flowers spilling all over the verandah, fruit ripening on the trees, and a porch swing. Delicious hot days were spent lying in the shade with lots of friends close by. We were quite content as we skipped rope, played jacks, and flipped through comic books we couldn't read. I loved the long dusty roads and the endless delights of walking barefoot; my hair was a brown nappy crown, my smile bright as a May day, as the hot Alabama sun laid a soft mantle on my shoulders.

We spent quiet evenings watching the sky redden and darken to black, waiting to be called in to the house by our mamas. Yeah, just simple pleasures so deep, the air seemed still and sacred. I never liked changes, so when Daddy told us we had to move because Mama was going to have a baby and we needed more room, I begged to stay with Grandma. My friends lived close by and life was no longer full of bogey-men and dark shadows chasing us. I was happy just where I was, and wanted to live right there. Mama looked hard and mean at me. "Cat, stop this foolishness, life can't always go your way, things will be fine."

There was nowhere else we could afford to go but the projects. Miss Lily's neighborhood was full of flowers and a yard soft with cut grass. We had gardens brimful of vegetables and quiet in the air. We loved feeding cracked corn to the chickens in the yard, and the sound of the rooster crowing at the break of day telling us all was well. Grandma stayed on at Miss Lily's until she could find her own home. Her driv-ing business was thriving, and she was busy day and night.

I was five years old when we moved to the projects — gray, one-story, paint-peeling shacks, row upon miserable row. Things wouldn't have been so bad, but Mama, the one who told us things would be better, started bawling, and the day became gray.

Yeah, we had to move from the magnolia-shaded front porch to the squalor of the projects, monotonous shack after shack, like a line of prison barracks, all run-down and lonely looking. All of a sudden we were surrounded by noise. The icebox sat on the front porch, and it was so exciting to hear the men drive up, jump off the truck, grab a chunk of ice with their metal tongs and sweaty, muscular arms, and drop the ice into its box. There were few windows, and we were defi-nitely on the poor side of town, but the price was right.

The kids my age were great, but some of the older boys and girls were mean to Bobby and me. They would chase us, threatening to beat us up, and made our life hell. The bigger girls would pull my long braids and call me "yellow girl." Bobby had the knack of avoiding trouble, but I would never back down. Even though I knew I couldn't win a fight, I'd pick up a stick or rock and go down swinging.

My brother avoided fights. His friends were well-mannered boys, just a few, but enough for him in the projects. Bobby was so softhearted — he never killed snakes or shot birds with slingshots. Daddy always taught us to love the birds and all wild animals. Bobby found a nest of baby robins that had fallen from their tree and landed in the bushes behind our house. Daddy and Bobby secured the nest to a tree branch and started feeding those babies with an eyedropper. We worried till those little birds, with their droopy eyes and hungry little beaks, started eating. We were happy they lived, but wanted to cry when we had to take them into the woods and watch them fly away. It took them a while to leave, because freedom seemed unfamiliar, but off they flew.

We heard babies crying way too long. Mama would stop her chores and declare, "I swear, somebody should be there to hold that child." There were many fights among the grownups, and razor scars were common — beautiful bodies scarred forever. The women would curse each other. Their hair was greased and shiny, but their lips were pushed out and looked cruel. Some of the mean-eyed men fought over the smallest things.

Single light bulbs hung from the dingy ceilings, and our small windows were too high to see out of. We never got used to the police patrolling the roads. Grandma said, "Cat, being poor can make women old way too fast. Hunger can slowly carve a man down to the flesh covering his bones, making his ribcage show." I noticed a lot of pregnant women and young children chewing limestone. It looked like they were eating white rocks. Mama said, "Cat, be grateful. Some people don't get enough to eat, and that rock has the minerals they need." The smell of garbage blocked the sweetness of the night, and the sounds of people arguing and laughing late at night made it hard for us to sleep.

Mama's gardens at Miss Lily's were gone, but she had to have a garden, if not for food, then for beauty. Mama did her best in that bare yard. Even before we moved in, Miss Lily and Miss Dora dug up plants from their yards. Buckets were filled with flower starts, and all their old lard cans held plants. Daddy hired Mr. Henry to drive over a load of good black dirt, giving Mama a garden to plant in. Daddy knew the way to make Mama smile. Her plants were her jewels, making our yard home to birds and bees. Mama always created beauty around us. She told me more than once, "Cat, always remember, flowers were created to awaken the beauty in our souls and food to feed our hungry bellies." Her flowers were like friends. Forget-me-nots blue as the sky welcomed the spring. Calla lilies like white trumpets waved from a bed of green. Ruby red and pink hollyhocks, standing comfortably by the garden fence, seemed like women passing the time of day. Humming-birds and lizards loved it there. Mama transformed our dirt-scrabble yard into a paradise.

Daddy woke us in the middle of a hot August night. "Bobby, Cat, wake up. Mama is going to the hospital to have your new baby, and Grandma is staying here till I get back." This was Mama's first time not giving birth at home with a good midwife, so we just sat up through the long night till Daddy came home and announced the arrival of Miss Betty Jo. That girl was born tall and honey brown, with an atti-tude, and a voice that roared. We loved her, just like a baby doll — till she screamed.

Mama used her magic and made our dingy project rooms warm and soft. Daddy painted the walls gold and soft white. Mama's homemade lace curtains, usually cream colored, invited the sun and moonlight in, filtering the golden rays before they dropped their liquid pattern onto the floor. Quilts covered us, each homemade from scraps of our out-grown clothing. Lace, cotton, organdy, satin, taffeta, scraps of plaid, tweed, our lives were sewn with a fine hand.

I remember Mama cooking black-eyed peas, standing in the door-way trying to catch a breeze when the sky held no hint of a cooling rain. Sitting at the old kitchen table, I was staring at Mama. Her hand was leaning on her hip, and her back was to me, so I couldn't see her eyes. The feeling drifting from her was pure magnolias and salty tears. What can you do, five-year-old brown girl? I couldn't figure out what she was looking at, as the clothesline was the biggest view right then, hand-washed clothes flapping in the breeze. Mama was humming softly, and Bobby and I knew she was having a hard day. Bobby was eight years old and wise beyond his years. Sometimes he would look at me, and I swear all the answers seemed to be in his eyes. He took my hand. "Let's go outside, Cat. Mama is worried about money again, and doesn't feel happy. Let's pick her a bouquet of flowers." We picked dai-sies and roses for Mama, shyly gave them to her, and warmth seemed to fill her up again.

I swear, from the first day we moved into those projects, Daddy was determined to get us out of there. This was Mama's dream and ours too. We weren't fighters, but the meanness seemed to rise up from the ground here. Frustration, hopelessness, poverty — we had to move. Mama did the best she could, but the yards all around were so neglected, filled with garbage, old busted furniture, no gardens, and not much hope. No, this just wouldn't do. Daddy got two jobs: janitor during the day, then painting till dark, saving enough to rent us a house, a real house with a yard and garden space.

It was the sort of summer day when even the hardest heart is moved by the beauty of the blue sky. The wildflowers were swaying and the air humming with the buzz of the bees. Daddy bounded into the house, eyes all wide, mouth big and grinning, "Get to packing, y'all, I got us a house on Peach Street with our name on it." Daddy worked painting houses for Mr. Daly. He liked Daddy's work, and asked if Daddy knew someone reliable to rent the house he was painting. Mr. Daly would trade work on the house for part of the rent. Mama started smiling, and her eyes filled with tears of joy. "God is good, children, God is good," is what she kept saying.

Even though we were moving to a new home, where Mama said the neighborhood was safer, I knew we'd miss our friends. The idea of not having Tillie down the road was scary. She was wide-eyed and brave and made me laugh, and her brother, Kali, was always keeping older kids from hitting me. Kevin was Bobby's best friend, and it troubled him to say goodbye to his marble-playing buddy. Even though we'd miss them, I knew we had to go. Mama kept saying, "Stop moping around, Cat, things will be better for us." But saying goodbye was no fun.

The afternoon we moved from the projects was hot and hectic. Mr. Harry's truck was loaded down with our beds and dressers, table and chairs, everything we owned. Grandma's car packed us in along with anything that couldn't fit into the truck. As we drove closer to the downtown area of Mobile, the dirt road became paved, and the houses looked bigger, with smaller yards and more people. Our new house wasn't fancy, but Mama and Daddy had their own bedroom. Betty was still a baby, and she and I shared a little room. Daddy made the back storage shed into a room for Bobby. He put in shelves for Bobby's books and his erector set. We even had a living room. Mama walked through the house humming softly, smiling. " J.C., look, there's a big front porch and a backyard big enough for a garden. I feel at home."

Daddy was our hero. His good looks kept Mama nervous. Daddy had way too many women admirers. We were proud of him for providing us with food, clothes, and a house. We had chicken for dinner most Sundays, and sometimes ice cream, hand cranked by us. The biggest thrill was when we got our own radio. We heard the news, music, soap operas, and the everlasting ball games the men listened to. All up and down the block during baseball season, you could hear the game from everybody's house. Things were looking up — Jackie Robinson was our hero, and Joe Louis was the world champion. In spite of the lynchings, burnings, and humiliations being part of our daily world, things were slowly changing.

Grandma couldn't read or write. She could sign her name on important papers, but that was about it. This was always an obstacle for her. She insisted upon school for us, helping pay our tuition. Grandma said she'd felt held back all her life. "Cat," she'd say, her eyes all dark and faraway looking, "To succeed in this world, you got to learn. This is a different time. I never had the chance to go to school, and you do."

I listened.

Grandma and her friends had wild imaginations. They believed in signs and omens. They seemed to enjoy reading tea leaves or each other's palms, trying to figure out who was going to get married, who not, who would live, and who would die. It was eerie how Grandma's eyes could appear to be closed doors though they were wide-open. Grandma said, "Fairies drink dew from the rosebuds, and sit in the green, shady parts of the yard. Those winged creatures can fly quickly lest some fox or cat or other wild animal strike them down. Fairies are here on earth to play, to sing and dance, and make us smile."

Grandma loved angels, too. She seemed to have inside information that angels were assigned to us at birth and stayed by our side all through our lives. Grandma had her own private place of worship, as she never went to church. In her room there were no crosses or pictures of Jesus, only angels. Her altar was covered in the whitest of linen, little rocks, dried plants, seashells, turquoise beads, incense, and always fresh flowers. My favorite object on her altar was the smooth porcelain statue of a brown lady with blue robes holding a dark-skinned infant. This Madonna's eyes were dark and serene, and she had a smile so gentle. She seemed to love the world and all its creatures. I loved that little lady. She was the only brown holy person I had ever seen. There were bird feathers, bones, little bowls of water, and always lighted candles in their glass holders. "Grandma's church," we called it.

Grandma and Mama couldn't have been more different. Mama was raised in the Baptist church, and Mama's rules were tight. Not so my Grandma. Her house was where I ran to and begged to sleep over, because the only rules Grandma had were easy: no fighting each other, and clean up after ourselves.

Grandma was deep and silent. She had the kind of face that seemed sculpted from red clay, then baked till it was coffee brown. Her African Indian face had high cheekbones, a strong chin, a full mouth, and piercing eyes. She held her body erect, as if she could take off running like a gazelle. Grandma always held her head up high. She looked like a queen to me. Like most blacks in those times, she was secretive. Rarely would she smile, only her black-as-storm-night eyes gave away her merriment. A big-framed woman, the lines on her face revealed her struggles.

Mama was pretty, like the wild orchids we find in spring. Her hair all shiny and pressed, she was a petite young brown girl turning woman. Her housedress hugged her little body gracefully. She loved telling us stories. Her beautiful smooth skin was shiny from the sunlight lying soft upon her. Those eyes could see right through us. Her mouth, still young and not disappointed looking, was full of hope and dreams. Her lips were like the red roses she loved. Sometimes her voice just drifted over our heads and we were warm and happy, like little puppies.

Mama was vocal. She sang all the time. I swear she was born with the kind of voice that is liquid gold, like honey after it's been left out all the hot day, a powerful voice, sometimes as soft as the baby she was nursing. I could feel her day through her voice. If she was overworked — too much laundry, not enough flour, rent due — she and the mourning dove could sing duets. On the power days, she could belt out the blues.

Grandma's baby brother, Uncle Roscoe, visited her every summer. He brought her a windup record player and records from New York and Los Angeles. He worked as a porter on the railroad, and when he went to New York, he would bring Grandma songs we never heard on the radio. When Mama heard Billie Holiday's song *Strange Fruit*, she started singing it, so beautiful, so sad. "Southern trees bear strange fruit, blood on the leaves and blood at the root. Black bodies swaying in the southern breeze, strange fruit hanging from the poplar trees." This song about lynching made our hearts silent.

Grandma Emma couldn't read or write too well, but she and money were well acquainted. She saved most every dime Shorty gave her. I heard Mama tell Miss Dora, "Lord, girl, Miss Emma got more nerve than any man. Here she is selling moonshine and holding poker games with her sister Sunny." Mama always tried to whisper so we couldn't hear, but we did. However she did it, Grandma saved enough money to put a down payment on a little house on Davis Avenue. Buy a house! That was a big achievement in those times. I always wanted to live with Grandma, but Mama wouldn't let me. Already Grandma was my champion, my defender, the spark that kindled my soul into believing that I was somebody special, could be anything I wanted to be, that I was a beautiful, brown little princess, not just another nigger child.

Mama would tuck Betty and me in at night and sing to us, "Hush little baby, don't say a word, Mama's gonna buy you a mockingbird. And if that mockingbird don't sing, Mama's gonna buy you a diamond ring." We were scrubbed clean, then dusted with talcum powder to keep the sweat down. Our nightgowns softly covered our young bodies. Our bed was made with soft sheets scrubbed white and then pressed with a hot iron so the cloth would feel soft. The things that love will do. Nestled under our homemade quilt, the world was ours.

The moon dropped in through the lace curtain for a visit; her gold dust touched our bed, and we cupped our hands to try to capture the light. There we lay, liquid gold on our shoulders, and love in our eyes.

Chapter 2

School Days, School Days, Dear Old Golden-Rule Days

The day finally arrived when kindergarten became a reality. Bobby was already in third grade, and he held my hand as we walked to school. I was scared, and didn't even dare to look at my new teacher. She was patient, and it wasn't too long that first day before I finally got up the nerve to raise my hand and talk to her. Her name was Miss Yvonne. When there weren't enough nuns, the school hired Catholic teachers. Miss Yvonne was young; her smooth black skin was like velvet. Her gold earrings shone in the light, and her lips were almost heart shaped. She was full of love, and seemed to know the hardships we were living. We were taught not to make fun of children with run-down shoes and secondhand uniforms. Some of the kids in our class appeared to me to be rich. Their parents drove them to school, and they were the first to make fun of anyone less well off.

I loved Miss Yvonne. She smelled like Mama's roses, and she opened the door to learning. I struggled to learn to color between the lines, and nothing was more fun than singing songs. The afternoons were gentle as we lay our heads on our desks and heard amazing stories read to us. Welcome to the world of make-believe. Miss Yvonne's voice was silky soft, and Peter Pan came to life, The Three Little Pigs, Hansel and Gretel, Cinderella, the Three Billy Goats Gruff, and Little Red Riding Hood. We loved those tales of magic, lost children, and animals that could talk. Kali was in my class, and we'd get into trouble giggling. I started picking the wool off my sweater and blowing fuzzy balls through the air. Kali followed my lead, and we both got a talking-to from Miss Yvonne.

We lived about two miles from our school. Bobby and I walked, skipped, ran, or played tag, picking up kids on the way to school. Life was sweet. I was proud to have a brand-new white uniform, new white socks, and shoes, my legs all greased down so they wouldn't get ashy looking, and my hair greased and plaited tight, secured by shiny barrettes. Mama packed lunch: baloney sandwiches, peanut butter and jelly, apples, and money for milk. Magnolia trees lined the roads, as did big, old water oaks, dandelions, goldenrod, and chicory. The birds were singing their hearts out. Honeysuckle vines trailed over fences, inviting us to pick their fragile flowers and suck the stamens' nectar.

Kindergarten was a world opening up. Words were being explained, and the alphabet was my favorite song. Grandma was proud of Bobby and me, and looked at our report cards carefully. Grandma paid the tuition for us to go to a Catholic school. She knew the nuns would not allow us to shirk schoolwork, and she kept stressing, "Learn all you can while you're in class, Cat. I never had the chance." The school year was fun. We played hard at recess time, and I had Charlotte, Kali, and Portia as classmates and best friends. Christmas and all the holidays gave us freedom, and we were already waiting for school to end.

Summer finally arrived, and the days stretched out endlessly, mosquitoes droning, chickens clucking, the old dog, Pal, our ancient German shepherd, slept the day away, too tired to chase butterflies or the neighbor's dog. Our cat lay motionless, liquid in the sun. The cry of babies, the creak of the old wooden swings on most porches, the hushed tones and gentle laughter of our Mamas because the day was done, dishes washed and dried, the world in order. Dream, dream, dream.

I lived for the start of another magical summer of golden lights and endless trips to the Gulf of Mexico or camping on the bay. Daddy, Mama, Grandma, Aunt Sunny, Uncle Rogers, and some of our friends, as many times as they could afford it, rented camping space on the colored beach. The men started wood fires and heated water in big pots to boil any crabs they caught, and to fry fish. We kids spent the days swimming or just lazing around, talking or singing, just peaceful. Our only job was to take care of the little ones. That was easy. Little kids calm down by the water. The last camping trip we took in August was different; summer was ending, and I knew school was next week. Bobby kept saying, "School days, school days, dear old golden-rule days, there's reading and writing and arithmetic, and don't get hit with the hickory stick." I just ignored him. School would be fun.

The school bell rang and another season began. First grade was different. This room had statues of the Virgin Mary and Jesus. Sister Agnes was my first introduction to a nun. She wasn't one to smile easy, and I missed Miss Yvonne. I used to try to get close to Sister Agnes to try to get a feel for her, but she only smelled like plain soap. The nuns' hot clothes and continual praying bothered me. I swear I wanted to run home. There was a big picture of a white man nailed to a cross. His eyes seemed kind and sad. There were thorns around his forehead, and blood was dripping down his lonely face. The picture showed his heart with thorns and blood around it. I couldn't help staring at that picture. Grandma had never told me about this man called Jesus.

We were introduced to Father Albert, a cold white priest who never smiled at us kids. He would be nice to Mama, but me, no. Welcome to catechism classes. Yep, from first grade on, we were introduced to guilt, the devil, heaven, and hell. Our schoolbooks featured Dick and Jane and their faithful dog Spot. Who were these people, all smiles, white, and happy? They lived in a big house and seemed rich. Their Mama wore high heels and an apron while she worked in their house. They were laughing at their front door, with a new car in their yard. This life looked so different to me. Mama never dressed up when she was home, and life wasn't so easy for us. That book showed me all the things we didn't have.

Grandma's little brown house on Davis Avenue was my favorite place to escape the madness of our home. Grandma lived six blocks from us, and walking there was easy. Mama had just given birth to Peggy, and the pressure was beginning to build. Mama had four kids now, and she had to work harder. Peggy was the light of my life. She was just like a real baby doll to me. She smelled new, and her skin was golden brown and soft as Mama's rose petals.

Mama started taking in laundry, hand washing, drying, and pressing clothes. We all had to help. Bobby was eight now, and I six; our chores were easy but necessary, so I loved to steal away to Grandma's house. She had the best place to relax, read magazines and ladies' style books, or just do nothing. I helped Grandma out from early on, so I guess I was kind of her pet. Grandma always warned me about dreaming too much, reading, not working, but I figured she loved it. I was always reading to her, best I could.

There is hardness to life that I couldn't understand. Lying on Grandma's luxurious rose-satin quilted bedspread, her soft pillows cushioning my fuzzy head, the world was a stage, and I, the fairy princess, was surveying my kingdom. It was a cold winter day, the sun hardly bothering to call. The sky seemed stark and gray, like just before the rains roll in. Just gazing through Grandma's polished windows onto Davis Avenue was not boring. On the contrary, people walked past doing errands, the grocery store, beauty shop, barbershop, fried-chicken joints, all on the same street.

It was late afternoon, the crowds had thinned, and only two black men were standing on the street, right in front of Grandma's house. I was almost asleep when the shouts began. Two young men were arguing. Both were cursing each other, their hands waving furiously. The anger felt like electricity, the vision burned into my soul. Two young men, neither could have seen twenty years, aggressive, hostile, dark-eyed men. One was short and round of body, his mouth seemed cruel, like not enough love was in his food. Maybe his mama left him early. His face showed the damage done. The other man had light brown skin, crinkly reddish-brown hair, and light-brown eyes that flashed danger. Although he was slight of build, his slender arms were quick to pull an ice pick from his waist and gash the other's face open. Across his cheeks, over his nose, then, fast as light, the ice pick flowed across his chest, a gash opened neat as a doctor's cut, the red blood did flow.

I screamed, "Grandma, help, a man is bleeding all over the ground." She heard me, and her big frame ran in quickly, pulled the shades down, and enveloped me in her big, soft bosom, all warm, smelling of rose water. By now the street was alive with people, talking quietly as they waited for a car to carry the man to the black hospital.

Why did they block the beauty of the day? Why did they hate one other? This was too sad for me. All I could figure was angels have a hard job loving their assigned souls, no matter what they've done. Grandma said, "The seeds of love are in everyone, but seems like life can be so cold, the soft of heart can weaken, and let the hatred chase goodness away."

I was six years old, full of laughter and dreams of falling stars granting wishes. I told Grandma later, after the police came and the men were taken away, "I wish life was like my fairy-tale books, and miracles happened like you say, Grandma." She looked me deep in my eyes, like she always did, and said, gentle as a morning breeze, "Cat, believe in the power of love and nobody will ever harm you. I swear your angel is there for you." This made me feel good, but the picture was burned into my head for a very long time.

Our school sat on Davis Avenue, a mean, run-down street, full of fading businesses and black-owned theaters that showed our own movies, black actors, beautiful brown heroines. Seems the successful black businessmen in the North realized the market for our own films. Daddy said, "Before talking movies, white people wore blackened cork over their faces to portray blacks, because we were considered too ignorant to act." Well, as the world turns, talking films came into being, and white people couldn't imitate our voices, so we got our first roles. Daddy would get so mad: "See, Cat? They give us the most awful roles. They always have us acting like ignorant, shiftless, servants."

We grew up watching cowboy movies: the Lone Ranger, the Cisco Kid, Tom Mix, and Zorro. These cowboys were killing Indians. We black kids, in our segregated aisles, cheered when the Indians were defeated. Whenever the boys played cowboys, I begged to play with them — after all, Bobby's friends were beginning to look cute. I was so desperate to play they always made me be the Indian. They would tie me up with clothesline and pretend to hang me. Why did we all want to be like the white people?

Daddy was controversial. He hated war, and said the Buffalo Soldiers, the black infantrymen, were praised because they helped conquer the Indians, helped kill the only true native people. My Daddy was a quiet man, a different man, never one to follow ideas he didn't believe in. His Daddy was German, and had talked to him a lot, and he had a different way of looking at things. He and Grandma never did go to church. Mama was raised religious, but never in our early days did she go to Sunday services.

It was the hottest of August days, the kind of weather that hinted of hurricanes. Probably it was just going to rain. The air was still, and the sky hung low, full of dark clouds. Mama and I both were dripping sweat. The attic fan gave no relief. Betty was hot and petulant, and Peggy was just lying around. Tired from doing laundry, Mama was just out of patience. When the knock on the door came, she looked out the little curtain and saw Mr. Johnson, the white insurance man. I swear everybody we knew had life insurance. I never could figure out why. Seemed it was always hard for Mama to pay the premium every month, but pay she did. Bobby said, "The only way Mama or Daddy could win would be to die."

I opened the door, and Mr. Johnson waltzed on in. Bobby and I hated this man. His walk was shifty, and his narrow, slate-gray eyes were mean looking. Don't know what came over him, but he threw his hat on Mama's bed, then proceeded to take her hand, and, leering, ask for coffee. I smelled the moonshine on his breath, and wished Daddy was home. Mama pulled her hand away, picked his hat off her bed, and told him to watch his manners. He practically yelled in her face, "Nigger woman, did I ask you for a damn thing? Hell, half these nigger bitches would screw me for their premium." Mama burst into tears and shoved him out our door. I felt kind of sad, but didn't understand Mama's tears.

When Daddy came home, tired and paint-stained from work, Mama quickly told him about her day. I just stood in the doorway, trying to understand. Bobby was holding my hand. Daddy was so mad his face got all red and his eyes were just slits. "I'll kill that cracker, I'll kill him dead." We quickly called Grandma to come over. Daddy didn't get mad too often, but when he exploded, watch out! He didn't say another word. After a quick shower, he was out the door. Mama tried to stop him — no luck. He was gone in a flash. Grandma came in soon after he left. Her face looked tired, like she had seen too much this day.

Heaven help us if Daddy went after Mr. Johnson. Daddy was a black man, and his complaints would most likely end up with him getting beaten and jailed. The night was inky black, and the waning moon hung red and gold. Mama didn't even tell Bobby and me to go to bed. The very air was static with fear, and we couldn't have slept even if we wanted to. I finally drifted off clinging to Grandma. The early morning light was spilling through the window, the night stealing away, when the police car arrived bringing Daddy home. He had drunk too much and passed out on the sidewalk close to home. The police gave Mama stern warnings of what would happen next time, and left. We were delighted Daddy was home. He was angry and hung-over, but alive.

Daddy had the gift of talking to birds. He'd always whistled, so it was easy for him. He said he started calling birds when he was little. Birds sang back when he answered their calls. Bobby and I spent hours practicing different sounds, trying to whistle like him. Many a person was fooled and thought Daddy was a bird. He loved the woods, and passed on to us that awe of nature. The earth comforted us; her strength pushed up through our bare feet into our souls.

Daddy's church was the woods. Our fondest times in the summer were spent with him, trekking though the swamps, careful to not step into quicksand by the creeks. I remember once stepping into the creek and sinking instantly up to my waist in the deadly sand. Terrified, the more I struggled the deeper I sank. Daddy pulled me out. Another lesson learned. He taught us to sit still as the deer grazed close by, all gentle-eyed and alert. If we made the slightest movement, they would dart away. Daddy said the calls of the blue jay let the animals know we were around. We would silently start walking into the woods, and the blue jay gave out his warning. We could hear the cries of the other birds traveling through the country announcing our presence.

The mockingbird sang the various calls of other birds as we lay on the grass and watched her sitting on the highest branches, singing melody after melody. Daddy could imitate the sweet notes of the little hermit thrush. We were content to spend hours in the deep coolness of the woods, as we silently ate our lunch while Daddy fished.

There we sat, silent in our sanctuary. We were at home among the wild things. We chased fat green bullfrogs croaking, trying our best to catch them. I was afraid of the king snakes slithering silently over downed logs, but Daddy would pick one up and let me hold it. He said, "Cat, this snake will never hurt you. Look close at the beauty of it's coloring. This is a creature of the earth just like you." That was just like Daddy. Part of him seemed like a child, always taking the time to show us the beauty of the earth. We were so excited to see foxes running close by, eating the scraps of food we threw into the bushes. Daddy showed us the tracks of bears, their claw marks shredding up tree bark or overturned logs where they grazed for grubs.

This was home to us; the deep, cool forest, the pines swaying in the breezes, cold springs giving us sweet, pure water. At sunset we sat watching the evening sky turning the clouds overhead into red, orange, golden lights welcoming the approaching evening. We loved twilight time. Our church was the earth and all her creatures.

How we loved those trips into the swamps and deltas with Daddy. Sometimes in the early spring Mama came with us to gather herbs for her tinctures. She sang to herself while she picked her medicines. Daddy introduced us to the comfort of green trees, young spring orchids, violets, and wild ginger plants. Mama taught us early the value of herbs for medicine. She and Miss Lily made tinctures and sold them, so it was business and pleasure for her.

Mama looked so soft in her summer dress and sandals, her face shaded by her wide-brimmed hat. She looked like a lady out of a storybook. The ground was an exquisite carpet of color. Bobby, Betty, and I sat silently enjoying the lights changing color on the water. Daddy was teaching Bobby to fish the bass-filled ponds. Yep, we didn't have money, but we had the earth and all her treasures.

The clear, light days of childhood call to me, voices on the wind, fairies in every flower. We wore daisy chains on our heads as crowns. In our world, all of us were princesses. Life was a rainbow bridge for us girls to span, where princes waited to rescue us. Our dolls were lots of times old Coke bottles with thatches of spiky, green grass jammed into the opening. For hours we would comb our dollies' hair, content in our world of light and shadows. Africa in our veins, oppression all around us, we played, happy, under the summer sky.

By the time I was getting on to seven, I began to see that we were poor. Daddy would tie his shoelaces together when they broke, so he didn't have to buy another pair. Our socks were darned at the heels so many times they got too thick to wear. Daddy would put cardboard inside his shoes when the soles wore through in places. This would have to hold him till he made enough to buy another pair. Everything was precious. I would ask Mama, "Why are some of our friends so dirty and their clothes raggedy?" Life was still magic, but I was beginning to feel poverty's sting.

There were children with no shoes, no daddies; their mamas were worried looking and tired from too much work. You could see how some of Mama's friends didn't laugh enough, or how they shyly put their hands in front of their pretty mouths. They were too embarrassed to have few teeth, or teeth so rotted sometimes only broken-off snags remained, brown and sad. Mama told me softly, "Honey, life is hard for a lot of us; all we can do is love, and share what little we have."

So many of my friends didn't have enough to eat. Mama always cooked extra because if any of my friends were over at dinnertime and looked hungry, she fed us all. I would watch her dividing the food carefully so everyone got some rice and beans, a little piece of a chicken wing, a sliver of pie. We all lived beneath the wings of poverty.

My earliest memories of Alabama are vague. The war was over, and blacks were getting jobs. Daddy complained there were no colored unions, which meant the whites working right alongside him were getting better wages for the same job Daddy and his friends were being paid pennies for. Daddy turned the anger he felt into working for the right to have a union. He and his coworkers held closed meetings at our house. The shades were tightly drawn, and we were warned never to talk about anything that happened. The march for freedom was beginning.

None of the grownups would talk to us about the troubles we were having. Mr. Taylor would come over and talk to Daddy. We were told to go outside to play, but we listened sometimes at the door. "J.C., times are getting more intense. The Klan is out riding more because we are demanding an end to segregation." Daddy would talk real quiet: "I'm afraid there will be more trouble than we can imagine." Crosses were being burned at any so-called troublemaker's home. The newspapers reported fire bombings in the night and brutal lynchings. How we hated the Ku Klux Klan. These were faceless cowards. Their eyes were slits through their masks, and they wore pointed hats with white robes. Daddy told us they were haters of black people, and considered us racially inferior.

I felt sad and confused, but the song sparrow sang to us, the willow trees danced in our honor, the sky kissed our brown cheeks, and we had each other. Never before had we begun to stand up in such numbers. Daddy said, "The fear of death is nothing compared to the horror of living forever oppressed." Fine for Daddy to say these brave words, but Bobby and I were afraid. Daddy thought we weren't being told enough about our history in school, so he was always adding to our education. He'd say, looking all serious, the sun making his eyes squinty, "Cat, we are, all of us, descended from Africa, yet we still imitate the old slave masters. We are ashamed of ourselves for not being white."

Whenever Daddy talked serious, we listened. He was teaching us to be proud. He told us that even the richest black kids had to go to the same run-down, old schools we did, go to black hospitals, drink the same colored water, and sit in the back of the bus. We couldn't vote, and definitely could not eat at Woolworth's or any restaurant not specifically for coloreds.

You could learn about oppression from looking closely at people, see the tired stoop of a shoulder after picking cotton all day, the weary smiles for your children after being a mammy for other people's children from dawn to early evening, no time to enjoy your home or the simple pleasures of watching your own a bit more. I could feel the silent anger coming from Daddy and his friends, much more than from the women. The black man was always in danger if he got uppity. Mama worked long hours, so our jobs were many and necessary. My job was to watch Betty and Peggy while Bobby finished cooking the beans and rice. I helped stir the cornbread while Bobby made the coleslaw. I set the table so that when Mama and Daddy came home all tired and grumpy, they could relax. My parents labored all day for pennies, Mama as a day worker, Daddy painting and doing janitorial jobs.

How hard can you squeeze a man? Stripped of dignity, how tall can he stand? Well, we were a testament to endurance. I remember the roads lined with the board houses we lived in. They were called shotgun shacks 'cause if you shot through the front door, the buckshot would go straight through the house. No matter what, it was home, and Mama's little touches made it secure for us. The scars of segregation lay deep beneath the flesh. Tales were told after we were supposed to be asleep, but kids always listen, and then dreams of terror and nightriders tear away the fairies and strip away our innocence.

I loved lying on the front porch swing, chewing gum, being quiet so as not to interrupt Grandma Emma and Mama shelling peas or shucking corn. Lying there in the shade, the only sounds were the rustle of the wind and the occasional bird chirp, as the sweet magnolias drifted heavy perfume over our heads. They were relaxed, and the stories about our relatives and friends we left behind in Mississippi flowed from their lips.

I listened as Mama softly talked about her daddy. "Miss Emma," she said, "times were so hard for us. You know my daddy was a handsome high-yellow man. He ran booze, and killed a man." I don't know if Mama knew I was there in the shadows, quiet as a mouse. Sadness in her voice, Mama said, "He escaped jail in Saint Louis, Missouri, and escaped to Detroit. Soon as he got established as a white man, he came back down to Mississippi and took Minnie and my baby brother Lonnie with him up north. They were fair enough to pass for white. He left me because I was too brown, and my Mama was already dead from a bad heart." Softly, Grandma said, "Honey, that's all right, your Aunt Hattie and Uncle T.C. loved you as their own, and we got to have you."

My brown little mama was abandoned! I sat there trying to be invisible, but the hurt inside of Mama came into me, and I wished I could hug all the sadness out of her. Mama never talked much about her past. She told Bobby and me that her Mama died when she was ten, leaving her and her brother and sister in the care of her mama's sister, Aunt Hattie, and her husband Uncle T.C. That's all she'd tell us. The more I begged her, sitting quietly on the porch at night, the more she'd close down.

A shadow seemed to cover her eyes. Secrets, secrets, what was she hiding? She never wanted to tell me about her past. Her mama, her daddy, her grandma, no, the past was just that with her, over, not to be talked about. After Mama married Daddy, Aunt Hattie and Uncle T.C. moved on up to Memphis and started work as live-in domestic workers. The pay was good, the white people kind, but Mama lost her only relatives.

Imagine the joy when Aunt Minnie, Mama's long-lost sister, arrived at our door. Curiosity all over my face, I said, "Mama there's a white lady asking for you, and a little girl, too." Welcome Aunt Minnie Rivers, hair dyed red as a flaming sky, skin slightly yellow, and eyes green-brown; pure glamour. My cousin Leslie came in after my auntie, and it was love at first sight. Leslie was my age, and a new best friend.

Detroit was big and fancy, so why did they come to raggedy old Alabama? I wondered. But there were never any answers. As soon as Aunt Minnie arrived in Alabama she figured out quick that there were no good jobs for coloreds, so she powdered her high-yellow cheekbones, put red lipstick on her full sweet lips, and curled her red silken hair. She wore her fine clothes from Detroit, and got a good-paying job at the big department store downtown. Of course, she had to pass for white, but that was easy, she had done it all her life.

Things went on well for a while, more money in the house, everybody settled. One day, though, maybe blame it on the intense August heat, the humidity, the sweat, lies, and deception, whatever the reason, one dark hot day, a saleslady started laughing at a little black lady and called her a nigger. Aunt Minnie blew; she pulled the woman down on that expensive carpet and proceeded to punch her face. They pulled Aunt Minnie off her and fired her on the spot. This marked the end of passing, the beginning of pride.

When Aunt Minnie came home we knew something was wrong.

Mama asked her, "What's wrong, why are you home so early?" Aunt Minnie said, "Mabel, I am tired of passing. I am proud to be a Negro; I just can't lie no more. Hell, I am home!" Mama was mad that Aunt Minnie blew a good job. Me, I finally had someone to believe in. Aunt Minnie was home, one of us, and damn proud. She thrived in Mobile, and soon she got a job as a receptionist for Dr. Gaines, with pay good enough to rent a little house close to us.

Leslie and I were laughing with joy. She would go to our school and be in my class. Aunt Minnie was the belle of the ball. Her Northern manners, fine clothes, and high-yellow skin ruled. The South was so confusing: the lighter your skin was, the better your chances to make it, get a better job, be the first pick of the men. Aunt Minnie was light skinned, so the high-society guys came a'courting.

It didn't take long before she hooked up with Dr. Bubbah Gaines. Mama was overjoyed. "Girl, you are striking it lucky. That man is rich and good-looking!" Aunt Minnie was his secretary, then his girlfriend. His was one of the high-class families that lived on St. Ann's street, where all the professional coloreds lived. This was the society of blacks who had Jack and Jill clubs for their privileged brats, debutantes, balls, ballet classes — you name it, they claimed it.

Faster than you could say jackrabbit, Aunt Minnie married Bubbah, one of the biggest, drunkest, lying doctors who ever walked the streets. He built her and Leslie a fine brick house, complete with maple furniture, couches, leather chairs, and thick rugs. Leslie even had her own bedroom, something unheard of to us. Welcome to the land of snobby people, who seemed to think their job in life was to save us, the uneducated masses.

We were never welcomed by that band of people, tightlipped Christians, college graduates, professionals, lots of them with light skin and good hair. Nappy hair and dark skin was just not in, 'less you had plenty of family money. There was a saying that I hated: "If you're white, you're all right, if you're yellow, you're mellow, if you're brown, stick around, if you're black stay back." My sisters and I were definitely confused; brown girls we were, curly-haired, light brown eyes, all the right ingredients to be favored, but just no money. Hell, I could care less; the cold stares of the high-class people among us made me long for my poorer friends who were not at all snobby.

Seems like I was about seven when the whippings started. When we were smaller, we were spanked on our butts, but not too hard, just enough to make us cry. But soon the new form of punishment changed to whipping us with peach-tree switches. I never did figure out why we got hit so much, not only us but most kids. No wonder I loved my Grandma so much — she never hit us. She would look real mean and warn us, "Straighten up or I'll take you home right now!" No, she never did beat us, but Mama and Daddy did. They believed in whippings. I swear the favorite thing seemed to be to whip us. This was my first spark of hatred for the hand that nourished and comforted us. Whippings for talking back, clothes not ironed properly, arriving home late, chores not done, you name it, I claim it. Spare the rod, spoil the child — the most hated saying to children.

I would always run away from Daddy's belt, Mama's switch; catch me if you can, which, of course, they always did. I remember how, after one of Mama's spankings, can't remember for the life of me what I did, my little soul felt bruised and hurt. The summer air was humid; the leaves on the bushes seemed droopy, and all my fairies were hiding far away.

I sidled up next to Mama, her body all tight and cold, wrapped my skinny arms around her waist, and with my heart in my eyes asked her, "Mama, don't you believe in fairies? I can see them resting under the shade of the flowers or near the edge of the woods. Grandma says the cool, dark ferns seem to comfort them. The cats see them and always are stalking them, but those fairies can fly away ever quicker than some earthbound cats.

"Mama, can't you hear the fairies sing along with the nightingale and the crickets? Grandma says they are gentle and they don't hit their little ones, they are here to protect us."

Mama would get so mad at me. "Dreamer, you are just one more poor-ass little colored girl, and ain't no fairies real." I ignored her because Grandma told me about the fairies and angels, and she didn't lie.

Mama had days when sadness seemed to envelop her. I couldn't figure anything out. I asked Grandma one Saturday as I was helping her fold laundry, "Grandma, does my Mama hate me? Did Mama ever really want to have me? She treats everybody else better than me." Grandma held me tight and said, "Cat, your mama is going through things you are too young to understand or do anything about. Yes, she loves you, she just has a lot of trouble with your Daddy sometimes." I didn't want to hear Grandma. I knew Daddy always had ladies calling him about working for them, and he stayed out way too late.

I wish I had been able to talk to Mama. All those starched hand-made organdy dresses, the handmade dolls, the quilted bedcovers, these things were her way of loving us. Oh, behold the fall, when the veils are split asunder. Mama's beatings were severe. I could have endured them if there were a tear, a soft smile of care. Instead, studied indifference blocked her soul, and the beaten child was left to whimper.

Tell me, Mama, who am I and what am I to be? Were you ever like me? Who was your mama? Did she hold you in the night? Did she defend you and make the demon things fly away? These questions were never allowed, but that was a long time ago, and I was way too young to know how to melt Mama's frozen heart. A shade covered her beautiful eyes, and we girls had only to wonder, holding each other in the night.

Despite our sufferings, we had golden days. We chased fireflies in the night and played endless games of hide-and-go-seek. There were black-berries to pick by the bucketful, as that was next winter's jam. When did our life really start to go sour? What really was to blame? Was it the failure to have the money to take us to the dentist when we had toothaches? Was it the anger at never really seeing a way out? What really caused the endless slaps and beatings? Why did the descendants of African people, known to be so kind, hit their children?

Bobby's friend Billy lived around the block from us. Billy was good at making up jokes. He was the only white kid we played with. He had freckles all over his sunburned face, red hair, and a happy smile. Of course he could be mean, too, because being the only white kid in the neighborhood could be trouble for him. Billy loved to whistle and fly kites with us. We rode his bike all over the sidewalks, and never thought much about his color. Billy and his family were the only whites remaining in our neighborhood. Seems as soon as blacks moved into an area, the whites panicked and fled, so it was only a matter of time before they would leave.

We played with joy and abandon, knowing in our heart of hearts these times were special. Soon Billy and Miss Wilma, his mama, would move to a land where we would never again play. Billy loved to watch clouds. He would climb into the low branches of the sycamore tree in his front yard and call me, "Hey Cat, climb up." We would watch the clouds drift by and see dogs and dragons, snakes and monsters. Billy was gentle, and took time to be kind to younger kids. Maybe that's why I loved him so much. Once, when I cut my finger, he put salve and a Band-Aid on it for me. He was like Bobby, just plain kind. I loved him.

Billy was really Bobby's friend. He was older than I was, but if my brother wasn't home, I would get to hang out with him. Only when I got older did I understand that white people who lived close to us were called white trash. What did they mean, white trash, when Billy's daddy worked as hard as my own and was never harsh with us kids? Daddy warned us, "Racism is a dangerous thing. It can start making sense to the ones who are prejudiced against, and breed the same hatred from one to the other."

Daddy explained why we were confused. We didn't have role models. He explained how we once were African kings and queens. He said our ancient history was destroyed by slavery. We were powerful people, figuring out the stars, the planets. Early in time we had sundials, and figured out how to plant and gather our herbs for medicine. Respect for the earth was our religion. Daddy said our ancient religions were destroyed, and we were denied the truths needed to help us know our history and our role in this country. I was too young to figure these things out, but my soul felt adrift. Sometimes I would get sad when Daddy talked serious to us. It was like he was pushing us too fast to know reality, and it scared me.

An owl lived in the woods behind our house. We could hear him calling at night and in the early, soft blue mornings. The sound stirred our hearts and brought to mind beauty and peace. He sat, talons tightly gripping the oak-tree branch, against the lacy Spanish moss, a thing of beauty with his unblinking, fierce, wise yellow eyes, his puffy, regal, tan and cream feathers, and his ruffled neck framing his fearsome beak. I'm sure the angels and fairies sat up there, too.

The owl is a comfort to a heart longing for freedom, a hunter. Distant, yet near, he speaks and the little things in the woods tremble. The children smile at the soothing call. When the owl called in the night from his tree, Peggy and I were often at the sill listening, trying our best to answer that lonely cry.

Welcome to the end of a long, hot summer. We have enjoyed watermelons, fireflies, frogs, crickets, birds, barbecues, and summer swimming at the public pool every minute we could. Welcome to reality, and enter the second grade. Our new teacher, Sister Vincentia, was tough as nails and skinny as a wooden slat. She seldom smiled, and I started to feel trapped. Even though we weren't baptized Catholics, we had to go through the Bible classes. All of a sudden Jesus is present, twenty-four/seven, and I'm not lying.

Our tender little hearts and minds are exposed to guilt. Catholic school was becoming a world of fear, heaven, glorious home to brave saints, pure nuns and priests, and very unlikely me. Hell seemed my destination; already the purity was being tarnished, rusted. The feeling of being trapped became a reality. We were told if our parents and friends didn't become Catholics and go to church, they were doomed to everlasting fire and smoke, doomed to burn forever. What a crock! I would come home from school and gaze at my Mama baking bread while she listened to her music and wonder how come she had to burn. Fear, terror, bad dreams, and we paid for this torture! I know Grandma thought she was helping us get a good education, but she didn't even go to church. Grandma said to ignore the religious part, just learn the book work. This was so hard for me. Bobby didn't seem troubled by the catechism classes, but I was. Bobby was already talking about becoming an altar boy and getting baptized. I was just worried about my soul burning in hell.

Wouldn't you know it? There's always the prissy, perfect kid in class. Bernadette was one of the holier-than-thou crowd — you know, the ones who the nuns are sure have a vocation, a calling to the Lord. Give it a break. I would always sneak looks at Bernadette's smooth brown face, long lashes and deer like eyes, and wonder why she seemed to be so holy among us bad kids. I couldn't figure her out. We were sure she was bad when we didn't see her. Being perfect seemed so unnatural; you know, over fervent at church, like a little holy girl, disdainfully looking over our sinful faces.

The night takes the blue from the sky, gold fades slowly from the hills, the days get longer, and new energy comes barreling in. I don't know how every year at a certain time, usually about the first week in May when the ground gets warm enough to crouch on and dry enough to draw circles, marbles appear, as if by magic. At a certain time we all go to our dresser drawers, shoe boxes, or any other stash and pull out our treasures — marbles, cat's eyes, your wealth strictly depending on how many marbles you have accumulated. I was a tomboy and played with a passion. Marbles were our joy. Kali was one of the best players in our crowd and took the time to show me how to shoot like the boys. That's why I loved him so much.

Kali was most definitely one of my best ever friends. Miss Dora had five kids when Kali was born sickly. He was the smallest of their brood; short, brown as roasted coffee, eyes black and deep, like a river under the shade of the overhanging trees where you can't see the bottom. I swear so much love surrounded Kali even mean kids would seem to soften, not hit him, and he just had a cloud around him, a cloak of goodness. Kali loved to play marbles too, and we would always share our stash.

Naturally I loved to play with him. He would listen to my many tales of woe and always manage to make me feel the world was really all right. Even though we were poor as church mice, Kali had a smile that a king would envy. Joy was born his companion. When I was feeling mean and low-spirited, Kali was there with the jokes, the slow easy smile that made my grumpy spirit feel like singing again.

Chapter 3

The House of Dreams

We have once again outgrown our house. Peggy, Betty, and I share one little room with no space for a dresser. Bobby still has his little room, but the time has come to move on. Mama and Miss Terrecina found us a house to rent. It was freshly painted yellow with green-trimmed windows, with a big kitchen and a backyard with a rope swing hanging from an old sycamore tree. There were flowers, and the yard was fenced, with a front porch. We had three large bedrooms and a dining room, too.

The house came with an old upright piano in the living room, and music entered our life. Mama's piano was a vehicle for her soul. Her smooth brown fingers found a voice, and the joys and sorrows of her life were felt through her singing. That short brown mama of four could sing sweeter than the hermit thrush, softer than the mourning dove. She could belt out the blues, lift our spirits, and soothe our souls.

Mama insisted I take piano lessons from Mr. Franklin, the gray-haired organ player in our church. Dread upon dread. I just wanted to play rhythm and blues, chopsticks, old spirituals, make up my own songs, but no. Mama insisted I learn writing and playing from Mr. Franklin, note by weary note, theory dulling my ear, shutting down my mind. I could pretty much hear the notes, play by ear; every tone held pleasure, a different hue, and shades of pain, joy, love, and sadness. My earliest memory is the sound of Mama singing. Wherever we lived, people sang together in harmony; on street corners at night, on front porches, we all sang, it seemed as natural as breathing. One thing about Mama, she didn't seem to care how hard it was to play music by ear, and she never appreciated my learning "Stormy Weather." She just wanted me to be more cultured, classy. Nothing wrong with that, I just wanted to play like Fats Domino, the real master to me.

I spent so much time practicing love songs from the radio, a note at a time, that I never had the lessons done, so I was dropped from Mr. Franklin's music classes. This was good for me. The boring habit of spending part of my Saturday wrecking Mozart's beautiful work and wasting Mama's twenty five cents was better off dropped. Nope, the world of culture was too far away for this blues-loving girl. But I learned the basic notes, and though I couldn't sing in tune to save my life, my piano playing got me into singing, because I could play the chords.

I loved our new house. I could walk to Charlotte's, and Portia lived two blocks away from her. We were still close enough to Davis Avenue to walk to school, and Grandma was right around the corner. Mama still had her sewing club, and the ladies sometimes brought their kids with them. When the group met at other houses, we would tag along to visit with our friends, even though most of us had younger sisters or brothers to watch while the ladies sewed. I remember drinking iced tea out of tall glasses with long glass stirrers for the sugar, and delicious pound cake served on little plates. The sewing circle was a good excuse to party for the young and old.

Our new neighborhood was a joy for us. I was still a tomboy, and loved to play softball with the girls and boys on weekends. We had a field close by, and the games lasted all through the summer. Plus, boys did fun things besides play with dollies. We built kites, played marbles, and raced a lot. I still loved my girlfriends, Charlotte, Portia, Tillie, Leslie, and my sister Betty, but sometimes boys just had more fun.

Ever met people who loved cats more than you? Miss Flora loved cats more than us kids. She and her sister, Miss Annabelle, lived across the street from us — two old maids, Mama called them. They weren't twins, but both were yellow skinned and stringy, with lovely brown-and-gold-streaked eyes, like amber. I swear sometimes they seemed to be living in another age. Miss Flora walks firmly, head up, aggressive, while Miss Annabelle kind of silently enters a room; you have to become aware of her presence. They lived distant, were high-class teachers, and owned their own home.

Their house was so beautiful, shaded garden paths on brick walkways, flowers perfuming the air, gardenias, violets, drooping wisteria, splendid in their purple glory, climb to the top of an old oak tree. High above, it twists and turns, up to the top where the nests are plentiful, like summer hats crowning the treetop. Bird songs fill the air. I loved this house; butter yellow with dark wood trim, a peaked roof, lead-paned glass windows, and shiny wood floors. It was magic to me, a place where the princess waits for her young lover to come, a porch shaded and cool. The only problem was, Miss Flora didn't like kids.

My bed was by a window that looked across the street into their front garden. I'd daydream I lived there and Miss Flora was my Mama — don't ask me why, heaven knows she didn't particularly care for me." Cat," she'd holler at me, "you been picking my roses again?" or "Cat, how many times I got to say don't come over when we're gone?" I'd listen, but not hear a word she said. Mama told me time and time again to just stay away from there.

But oh, no, I always felt I had lived there before; even the scents from the garden were always in my mind. That old porch swing was heaven, soft red pillows, so fine to read a book or just lazily pass time swinging, quiet comfort for a young heart. When I ran away from the clatter and rattle of my frantic, kid-filled house, that yard was my spot, so I was determined to win Miss Flora over.

The best way to get to her soft spot was by being nice to her cats, 'cause she did love those killers from hell. Miss Flora sometimes looked worried, crease lines on her forehead, her mouth a little sad, like a child after Mama has gone to work. When I looked deep into her eyes, which she didn't like, I'd feel like the sun was softer, the air sweeter, the day held promise. Her eyes gave her away. She never encouraged me to just visit. I worked for them twice a month cleaning, so the door opened and I came on in. I loved that house.

Miss Annabelle was quiet, soft spoken and held traces of the past around her eyes. Miss Flora, on the other hand, was loud and full of wit. It took a while before she melted, but I just hung on. I saw into her soul. I detested her plain gray cotton dress, her curly brown hair pinned tightly into a bun, and those plain black shoes. I always wanted to dress those sisters in red, gold, lavender dresses, with their hair flying free, and pretty patent leather pumps shining on their feet. No way, they dressed like they wanted to not be seen.

Miss Flora's cats, Pippin and Blue, were blue-eyed, white, fuzzy, fat killers, calmly playing with birds, snakes, and mice before they ate them. My favorite thing to do was to rescue the birds, the wild things. As those cats stalked the animals, I stalked them. I'd lie quiet behind the hydrangea bushes, silent when I saw them stalking. Just as they'd pounce on some hummingbird, I'd pounce on them. To the victor go the spoils. I'd free the mouse, snake, lizards; whatever they had pinned. I'm sure all the animals in the neighborhood loved me. Of course, as soon as those cats saw me, they were none too happy. Miss Flora had no idea about her cats and me. They weren't able to tell her.

As winter leaves and spring arrives, promising hot days and diamond nights, lazy naps and cool swims, Miss Flora melted. She began to call me over," Cat, got a good book for you to read." She'd call and I'd smile. None of the kids could figure out why those mean old yellow women were kind to me. I knew why, but they were my own friends, best kept that way.

I think most everybody I knew in kid land had a picture of an angel somewhere in his or her house. We had a print of an angel, sweet and soft looking, watching over two little children, a little girl about six, and a younger boy, getting ready to cross that old bridge, some of the slats were rotted off and the raging river roared underneath, dangerous scene. That angel was right behind them, her wings seeming to hover over their bodies, like feathery arms. Behind her were the deep woods, before her were those children crossing that scary bridge. Faith, love, and protection is what that picture portrayed to me.

I was so smitten with angels, why, I could see them in the most outlandish places. Their faces would be in the sky at night, stars and planets. There were angels in the flowers, wearing jewels in their hair, laughing with the fairies that inhabited our childhood world, that land of lights and magic. My Grandma said, "At birth we all have an angel to guard us, stand by us, love us." She said the bridge in the picture was slippery and broken like life sometimes could be, but in the hard times we had that angel and each other to hold on to. I always thought Grandma was an angel living in a woman's body. She seemed to know much more than any nun or priest.

I loved our new neighborhood. Nobody was rich, but the houses were well maintained and the neighbors were mostly friendly. We were so delighted that we lived next door to Miss Lynette and Papa Dee. Mama and her hit it off at once. They both loved to sew their own clothes, embroider, and sing. Miss Lynette was tall and almost skinny, and her brown skin was freckled. She had light brown hair that caught the red of the sun in it, and it was never straightened, so it seemed to curl around her forehead, escaping from her long braids. Miss Lynette had the warmest eyes, like looking into a pool full of little fish and water lilies. Her mouth was mostly smiling, and her voice sparkled like water when the wind whips it.

Her husband, Papa Dee, was a retired longshoreman, and their house held things from around the world. Why, Papa Dee had been to Africa, and was proud of our ancestors. He had carvings, cloth, and beads, things we never saw. Papa Dee was big and tall, with a stocky body. He wore faded blue overalls when he worked in his yard, and we could hear his loud voice singing. He was soft and kind to kids. They owned a big two-story house, painted white with grass-green trim. There were big azaleas, roses, figs, peaches, pecans, and a sitting bench in the backyard. The mourning doves cooed through the day, making the yard relaxing. We spent hours swinging on their porch, and the yard was usually filled with us kids.

Neither of them was young. They had three grown-up kids who had moved away, so Miss Lynette and Papa Dee began to take in foster kids. Their house was so big that by the time their children left, they must have been kind of lonely. After all, they had more love in them than most people I had ever met. So many of Mama's friends had fancy hair, and I always remember their long, sharp, red fingernails. A lot of those ladies treated us like we were insects, but Miss Lynette would call out in her soft as night voice, "Lemonade everybody, come on y'all. My cookies are ready, anybody hungry?" We spent so many lazy afternoons in the shade there.

The radio was always on, and the blues and soul music caressed our young souls. Miss Lynette brought Lula May and Maya home with them from the courts, and I was enchanted. Lula May and Maya were her new daughters, and we had two new friends to play with. Lula May was almost nine, and Maya, Betty's age, so new friends were our gift.

As fall approaches and summer turns her back on us, we reluctantly put away our shorts and sandals and return to prison — school I mean. Third grade had prepared a dreadful religious class for us. We were now seriously introduced to confession, limbo, and purgatory. Limbo, the place your soul goes to after you die and are not forgiven your sins. Your soul floats in space — in purgatory, the nun called it — dreadful world, and fearful nights. I swear, nine years old, and already they have me burning in hell! Seems like every damn thing we did was a sin: eating meat on Friday, sin; pulling our panties down for the boys to see us, sin; kissing softly under the trees, sin; lying, skipping church, sin; gambling for money, a sin. Everything we did was bad, not to mention Grandma's house of gambling and fornication. Holy moly — my family would burn for generations.

That school was like a mental prison. Never ask a question, just accept that these nuns, all dressed in their black-and-white, hot, sweating habits, know the truth, and were sent by God to save our ignorant souls. Way in my heart I knew there must be a better way, better answers, 'cause otherwise I was bad and doomed to hell. If fun was bad, so was I.

My classmates were the greatest thing about school. Conrad was my book-reading buddy, and Lamar was our rich friend who invited us over to his house on Saturdays to play in their big yard, complete with swings, slides, and a basketball hoop. Corrina was delicate and couldn't play hard because she had asthma, but I loved her. We sat around playing Monopoly and card games, or dressed our paper dolls. I swear I loved playing with both boys and girls. Mama preached, "Cat, you are too much a tomboy, start acting more like a young lady." I just ignored her. There was some streak inside me that just didn't want to be told how to act. Maybe blame it on Grandma, who encouraged me to win at baseball as well as play girl games. Life was fun, and I wanted to enjoy it all.

Charlotte, Portia, Leslie, and I were rebels, and were already considered troublemakers. The schoolroom was hot, and time stretched out endlessly. School lessons were easy for me, giving me time enough to get into trouble. I was so bored. The history lessons were never enough facts for me, and questioning the books was taboo. Daddy had already told me George Washington had slaves, and we weren't considered citizens. The Constitution said all men were created equal, except the Indians and us. Daddy questioned our books, and I would quote him in school and be reprimanded, never any explanations, just told to be quiet.

It was mid-February during the winter frosts, with icy roads and long silent nights. The black and lovely skies with the silver stars dominated the heavens at the dark-of-the-moon time. That February night death was out riding the back roads as the children all slept deep and peaceful.

Miss Alyce was Mama's best friend; they loved each other as sisters. They listened to soap operas together, did laundry, giggled and gossiped, hushing when we entered the room. Miss Alyce was married to Mr. Alonzo Thomas. She was soft and biscuit brown, eyes wide open and amber colored, slim and tall and she reminded me of an Egyptian queen with her high cheeks and hawk-like nose. Mr. Thomas was dark skinned, tall, a black-eyed man with dimpled cheeks and he wore thick glasses. You know — the kind of man who laughs easily and bends down low to hear what a child has to say.

He worked weekdays as a carpenter, but on weekends his guitar would come out and he would play the blues. He and his band would gig the city and rural juke joints. This gave him extra money and great joy. They had a little house down on Bayou La Batre, the place by the bay where colored people lived. We spent many happy summer days there. Days we swam, while the grownups fished. The men boiled big pots of water for crabs. We had fifty-five-gallon barrels of ice filled with soda pop and watermelons. The grownups played bid whist card games while the music played.

As fate dealt her cards that February night, when the roads got icy, Mr. Alonzo didn't turn up at home. Miss Alyce was frantic, she sent her brother over to get Daddy to help find him. Daddy and her brother, Mr. Daniels, traced his route home. Searching from the country road to his house, they found him almost home. The skid marks showed where his car slid off the muddy embankment, but only Mr. Alonzo's body was left, his soul escaped. In a puff of smoke, a wink of the eye, the joy left our neighborhood, and the wailing began. Miss Alyce, the prettiest lady I knew, Mama's singing friend, was crumpled, left with six children,

We were all young, I was nine, but death presented her ugly face to us, fearsome and all-powerful. To behold Mr. Thomas all dressed up with no place to go, laid out in a coffin in a suit I never did see him in, all powdered and made up; nope, this was something my eyes did not want to see. This coffin struck fear into the hearts of all of us children, but then again, we were young and that seemed a matter for grownups. At the church the black women were wailing so grandly, fainting, sobs, loud shouts, drama, and acceptance, home to the ancestors.

The men were all solemn, looking out of place in suits, passing whiskey around. The children generally had as much fun as possible at a funeral. Mr. Thomas, all pressed and powdered, held wonderment for us children, and for months afterward the memory held us, discussed at night when we felt restless or sad.

Along comes May, when the chinaberry trees begin to leaf, lilies pushing up, the huge hydrangea bushes with their big leaves, in the rain we would hold them over our heads as our little umbrellas, the lovely flower begins to swell, pregnant with her florets of petals, first white, then slowly adding lavender then blue to her color. May arrived, urging us to leave school and ride bikes all day, climb trees, and begin to seriously get ready to build our kites.

We used to buy the kite sticks and construct our own kites, glue the paper onto the frame, purchase the twine and fashion the tails from rags. Kite season was definitely a pleasure. The joy of us friends on the sunny meadows, breeze swirling erratic as we struggle to get her aloft, then joy upon joy, just holding that string and guiding our kites through the currents was fun.

When I was ten, Mama left home for twelve weeks. We were told she had a nervous breakdown. Peggy, Betty, Bobby and I knew Mama and Daddy were fighting a lot, so naturally all those tears wore her out, wore us all out. Mama had just six months earlier given birth to Linda, and things seemed to get bad for her. Daddy started staying out late at night and Mama was crying more. All of us older kids tried to shield newborn Linda from the chaos. When Grandma drove Mama to the hospital with Daddy accompanying them, we kids stood in the doorway, lost, feeling abandoned. I was too sad and scared to cry, plus Betty and Peggy were holding on to me for security.

Daddy hired Miss Terrecina to cook and help us keep the house in order. Miss T., as we called her, was our angel come to life. Mama left, Miss T. came in, brushing away our tears and sorrows. Those old hands kneaded bread firmly, wiping her hands on her apron, she'd look down and smile at us and the kitchen felt warm and smelled like fresh baked bread. The only sounds were love; the drone of the bees, the afternoon calls of the robins. Shafts of golden light streamed in through the window by the sink.

Those old hands of hers, wrinkled with brown age spots, could make a damn good cake. She didn't use the metal butter cutter. She always mixed the butter and sugar by hand, adding the flour and eggs without a recipe, perfect. Those old hands knew where the hurts were, and always took time to give us hugs; gently she kissed the tops of our heads, and the world became safe again.

When Mama finally came back home, she was so skinny. Her eyes looked just about cried out, like there wasn't any more water in them. Hard to explain, she looked so delicate to us, we were unnaturally good and extra-careful not to disturb her and let her heal. She was the only Mama we had. There were things we couldn't understand; there were secrets that were kept from us. We could feel the stares of the neighbors. My brothers and sisters were the glue that held me together, and I'm sure it was the same for them. We really only had each other.

I can't leave out my cousin Leslie, aunt Minnie's daughter and our first cousin, close as you can get without being real sisters. Leslie was white as snow, straight hair, light brown and silky, eyes blue as a spring morning, and a smile a mile wide, my cousin, so different from me. Leslie and I bonded instantly, another troublemaker, heaven. She was like my sister Betty. Leslie was born a businesswoman. One fine April day, she found an old rusty stake in the backyard. She was determined that it fell off the cross that Jesus was crucified on — holy cow, holy stake, what a moneymaker!

Leslie innocently asked Mama for a piece of satin from her sewing scraps, came outside, and laid the stake on the cloth, instant holy relic. We did this secretly. Way in the back yard we hung a sheet between two trees and immediately had Betty and Linda spread the news through the neighborhood that for five cents you could see the holy stake that killed Jesus, and for another five cents you could touch the stake for magical powers.

The news spread quickly. I was the collector of the nickels, and Leslie let the kids in one by one to view that sacred scene. We were so cruel, if you didn't have the nickel or anything to trade, like yo-yos, marbles, old pocketknives, kites, cards, slingshots, comics, fishhooks, you name it, we'd barter, but, no money, nothing to trade, you couldn't see the miracle, no mercy from us.

The line grew long into the afternoon, and we were raking in the cash, glory be, but as milk goes sour in the heat of the day, so did our business. Some irate neighbor called my mama and we were immediately shut down, told to give all the money back, and pray that God would not take us to hell before evening for such a great blasphemy. We got whipped, and didn't give back a penny. We figured if we got whipped we'd earned that cash.

Leslie looked so white that at school sometimes she was tormented, her long hair pulled hard, called cracker, peckerwood, white trash, so me and my army of brothers and sisters defended her, and our family ruled, 'cause there were too many of us to beat up. Mess with her, get three more, so things cooled down. She was still just another colored girl. Never knew anything about Leslie's past. Aunt Minnie just showed up one day with her, moved in and life went on. There were never any explanations and Leslie never talked about her past. The more I asked, the more she would look worried, and so I stopped.

I never could figure out why Aunt Minnie, Mama, and all their friends wanted fox stoles. All of them were crazy, I thought, to wear those dead foxes all sewed together, around their necks, kind of sliding over their shoulders. They swore they were the very height of fashion. Mama would smile at her sister and declare, "Girl, we are looking good!" They wore gloves, handmade suits, fancy hats, and dead foxes.

It scared me to see those little beady glass eyes, pointy faces, and sharp nails, brutal. When in reality, nothing was finer than seeing a fox, all reds and browns, streaked with gray. His bushy, shiny coat was grander than any old dog's. Foxes meant freedom and beauty to me, grandly posturing by the garden, on the edge of the woods, never too close, wild, untamable, the Creator's pet.

I remember Miss Brazil, our fifth-grade lay teacher. She had a big tall body, and her powdered, rouged old face was not a pleasant sight. Miss Brazil was about sixty, and didn't like to joke. Her mouth seemed to be turned down, and her nose seemed to always smell something unpleasant. Oh, brother! Her hair was straightened and dyed jet-black. She would look down on us; her thick glasses perched on her nose, and tell us, "If y'all don't straighten up, you'll be just like the Hottentots and bushmen you came from, ignorant and wild." I'd feel so bad. All of us had Africa in our veins, including her. My mama never told me this was a curse, so the rebellious me thought, "Shut up, old lady!"

Clarence, one of my best friends was black as night and handsome as any boy ever created. From the earth he rose, beauty in his swift movements, and a voice that could make birds envious. He always sang to me, actually to anyone who was near. "Beautiful, beautiful brown eyes", he'd sing and the earth stood still. He was my first crush. Those were stars, cotton candy, and honeysuckle days. He was the best at basketball and track and kind, kind, kind.

Whenever Miss Brazil made her remarks, I would look at Clarence and see the shame come over his sweet black face. His hair was short and nappy, with his flat nose and full lips, he looked like an African.

This woman was making him and all of us ashamed. I complained to Daddy how Miss Brazil made us ashamed of our looks. Daddy said, "Look hard at me, my Daddy was white, and I'm still just another nigger. Color doesn't matter, everybody's blood runs red."

Our class was black, brown, and yellow, green-eyed, black-eyed, and brown-eyed, all shapes and all colors. How many times were we taught by this black woman how the heathens in Africa were these coarse-haired, dark-skinned, ignorant savages? How is it possible we survived this kind of abuse? Actually how many of us really did?

Miss Brazil made me feel strange about myself and how I looked. I would come home from school and stare into the mirror, deep into my own eyes and then look at my brown face. My lips were big and my nose was flat, not straight, my cheeks were wide, and my skin was just plain old brown. I would always look through our geography books, through pictures of Africans, trying to find me. I just didn't feel pretty. I think once I found a picture of some island children, maybe in Samoa, and one little girl looked like me. I wanted to tear that picture out, but I couldn't. We didn't own the book.

Charlotte, Tillie, Leslie, and I were lazing away a Saturday afternoon, sitting on the front porch, repeating all the sayings we picked up from the streets. Charlotte and I started saying, "What's the word? Thunderbird. What's the price? Thirty twice. What's the reason? Pretty pleasin'. Who drinks the most? Us colored folks." Unknown to us, Daddy was painting the back porch and just listening. Next thing we start reciting, "Acka backa soda cracker, Acka backa boo, if your Daddy chews tobacco, he's a dirty Jew."

Daddy ran from the backyard to tell us how evil were the words we were repeating. I just started crying as my friends went home. I didn't know what a Jew was. Daddy told me later that evening, after dinner was over and he had cooled down, how these sayings were just making fun of blacks for drinking cheap wine, and he told me how millions of Jews were murdered in Germany. I swear my Daddy was my real history teacher.

There was one special nun we all loved: Sister Mary Margaret, our sixth-grade teacher, young as a spring day. Her skin was like creamy roses, and her eyes held merriment, joy, and mischievous laughter. And lo and behold she was a nun, a bride of Christ. Every now and then, I used to visit her in the convent on a lazy Saturday afternoon. They lived in a barrack-style house. It was clean — I'm talking so clean the floor almost squeaked — no cobwebs, no streaks on the mirror, no nothing. Their beds were skinny and made up tight, the walls were all white, and each one had a crucifix hanging over the head of her bed. The windows were small, and everything was painted flat white.

I would help Sister Mary fold mountains of laundry. They wore white boxer-like shorts and plain white cotton bras, absolutely no lace. It gave me the shivers sometimes to imagine living so strict, but she was my friend. I always tried to imagine Sister Mary running away one dark, starless night, hitchhiking on the side of the highway, her robes all taken off, and she looks all normal, her hair wild and free, and in the hot afternoons stretching her legs and arms out to the sun, 'cause they must be some kind of pale, being in that habit all those years. In reality, with the sun sliding down her lovely face, on those lazy Saturday afternoons, she would tell me of her childhood, innocent stories, but I always imagined only a deep dark tragedy made her choose this army life.

Sister Mary told me about Wisconsin when she was a child, green lands, lots of water, dairy farms, simple farm people, but she never met a black person till she went away to college. My guess is she thought she would be Joan of Arc here in Alabama, defending black people, leading us out of the darkness with the Bible to save and educate us.

She had the right heart, just somehow the same church she wanted me to praise shut her up about civil rights issues; any issues dealing with real times, these times, not Adam and Eve times, were not allowed. Our classes never stressed equality, like it was a given fact we were unequal, end of story.

Sister Mary backed me up. She seemed to understand my reluctance to be quiet, 'cause after all, how can you entrap an educated person, a reader, a seeker of truth? I don't know, but our school sure did. I learned to read early, and I loved it. The library was my second home. My favorite times were when I could stay at Grandma's house. I'd curl up in her bed and read. It was my escape, my way of seeing other worlds, hearing people think like I did. Books saved me. Sister Mary always encouraged me in following my dreams. She gave me a lot of books: Mark Twain, Ida B. Wells, Harriet Tubman — women and men who wrote about freedom and equality. Sister Mary was passionate about civil rights, but was in a church that chose to remain silent. Any thing I couldn't understand in my books, words unknown to me, Sister Mary helped me and gave me my own dictionary. I swear she was part black.

I personally hated the pledge of allegiance we had to recite every morning at school with our hand on our heart. Give me a break. Here we are all fresh, uniformed, hair greased and plaited, shoes shined, in some run down segregated school, on some clay road in the poverty belt of the nation, and we pledged fidelity.

Grandma prospered in Mobile, and soon bought herself a Chevrolet. She would let Daddy take us on Sunday after dinner drives. Oh yeah, we'd drive through neighborhoods full of mansions, complete with little black statues in the yard. Spanish moss draped from ancient oak trees and azaleas, brilliant red, scarlet, salmon, every hue of color were waving in the afternoon breeze. Magnolia trees perfumed the air; arrogant tree really, stands apart and wears the most garish white flowers, with the scent of pleasure, in her big leafed hair.

One lazy Sunday afternoon, we cruised way into the country, red clay earth. The chain gang prisoners were ahead. Police guards, wary and armed, patrolled the road. The prisoners seemed to be in a movie. The day was blazing hot and both the guards and the men looked soaked through with sweat. The convicts wore black and white uniforms, and could almost be clowns if they had red wigs and painted grins on their faces. The sun was blazing hot, and the highway a mirage as the horizon kept waving and disappearing.

These men worked swinging pickaxes — blacks and whites, whoever fell between the cracks in Alabama was in for a big surprise. The singing as they worked was powerful, that gift from Africa that made work a sad, strong song on the side of the highway, sweat, agony and the physical presence of captivity.

On one of our Sunday drives, Daddy took us way north into the woods and farmlands. The rows of cotton stretched as far as we could see. No, for real, these things do exist. The pickers dragged their bags behind them, sweating in the hot sun, fatigue all over their faces. Many a hand was bloodied from the cotton boll, the prickly crop.

Bodies were swaying in the sun. They had to fill that bag and live another day. The singing in the fields in the early part of the day, before the moisture from the night had been dried up, was bright and hopeful. Later in the day, with blood on their hands, the workers sing, almost dreamlike, a moan, a prayer, a tribute to the will to survive.

Heartless captivity. Daddy told us about an old man he used to see cooking in the Mississippi jail when his daddy was the sheriff there. Daddy would drop by the jail to get school money from my grandpa and was struck by the sadness of this old bent man. He was a white fellow with watery eyes and stringy muscles. Daddy said all the muscles developed over the years of working were just strips under his old skin. He said his daddy felt sorry for him and wanted him to be free. Daddy said the meanness in him had been long-ago gone, eroded by time and solitude. He murdered a man thirty-five years ago in a fight, and ever since has hung on the cross of redemption. He just wanted to be free before he died. He's too old to work the highway, so his cell is his home

Daddy told us tales of the South when he was young; the night he was too late for the curfew. Back then they had a curfew for colored people, you had to be in your neighborhood by eleven, or you were beaten or arrested. Daddy said, "There I am, my hair all wild and stringy, and my buddies and I are drunk as skunks, from drinking cheap moonshine."

They were out way too late. The police car came cruising down the dark street, spotted the four of them, stopped the car, and ordered them to stop. Everybody ran a different way. Daddy ran through somebody's backyard and almost got away, but the neighbors clothesline cut him off at the neck, and down he went. He was taken one more time to jail. Luckily, all of his friends got away, because they would have been beaten.

Back then his Daddy was the sheriff and he was let off, but none of them forgot. Yes, in the south you had to walk light, always look down when whites were approaching and certainly move over so they didn't have to touch you. Daddy told us how the Klan's men would lynch a black man and make sure his body hung all night and day, made sure everybody saw him. My poor dad, his face would get so sad when he told us tales of his past, of poverty, and racism, just to teach us, he said. Yeah, we listened.

My Grandma Emma would tell me the story of wanting to read so badly. She was born on a plantation, she and her sisters, born to work. The plantation owner's daughter, Jenny, I think was her name, a little strawberry-cheeked, golden-haired girl, her eyes blue like the sky, wanted to teach Grandma to read, 'cause they played together since they were born. In the late afternoons, under the big chinaberry tree, she and my grandma would begin the job of reading and writing. This went on for as many moons as it took old Miss Polly to discover her fair-haired daughter teaching the nigger girl to read, end of friendship, end of a dream for my grandma. I was crushed when Grandma told me this tale, and firmly vowed to learn all I could, 'cause books told me about other worlds.

Lonnie and Albert were new friends of ours. Albert was Bobby's buddy, and Lonnie and I were fast new friends. They lived down the street from us. Their mama, Miss Beatrice, was Mama's sewing partner. They sewed clothes for people, personally made to fit them from the pattern of their choice. Miss Beatrice was a Christian, and they didn't go to Catholic school, which I envied by now. Their public school seemed more fun, also more into having civil rights meetings to organize protests against segregation. Lonnie, Charlotte, and I loved to hang out together. We all played on the softball team, and after school we read comic books, played cards, and just enjoyed life.

I was starting to get it straight. Daddy and Grandma's stories helped me see the truth and understand the hurt inside my chest. We were told to never answer white men who drove by us in cars, because the Ku Klux Klan was out and up to no good. There were more and more meetings about equality, and the racial tension in Alabama was hot. When we got old enough to recognize colored toilets, realize we had to ride in the back of the damn bus, and accept that we couldn't vote, the bubble of childhood burst and the truth flamed up at us. We had no rights, no rights at all, just the privilege to work hard all our life and not expect too much in return.

Eleven years old and I am full of wonder and magic, piss and vinegar. The thought came to me that time was passing by, season to season, moonlight to sunshine, winter blues to summer ecstasy. Silver lights sparkled off the bay on a hot day, and the water was full of sparkling diamonds. I wanted to remember Mama's cooking, my baby sister Linda growing up. Grandma's hair was starting to show gray, which of course she had dyed black, and she would get it pressed and waved religiously.

Time talked to me, and I decided to capture the essence of that hot summer day. I wanted to remember the sound of kids playing off in the distance, laughter ringing through the road, the vegetable man in his old truck driving slowly by calling out in his singsong voice, "watermelons, watermelons, tomatoes, tomatoes, five cents a pound, ten for a dollar." He would sing out his wares, a different tone and melody for each vegetable and fruit. The dust motes in the shafts of light in the room, the drone of the bees, the chirp of birds, I just wanted to freeze time, one minute in my heart to never forget, and I haven't.

Mama always cut magnolias, gardenias, jasmines, camellias, they were always floating, the magnolias in glass bowls, whatever we had, old mayonnaise jars, anything to capture the beauty, to enjoy, to smell, to dream. The camellias were so bold, reds, pinks, creamy whites, they always reminded me of oriental ladies, beauty, the night-blooming jasmine flooding the humid evening air, filling it with overwhelming fragrance.

I used to tell my little sisters wild and wonderful tales of princesses and handsome knights, the fat man and the skinny woman, ghosts and witches and curses given by the evil ones. I would do anything to ward off the crying of my mama in the living room. I was the oldest girl, and Bobby and I knew Daddy was staying out way too late, or the light bill was due, or any of many problems. I would do anything to let them know that life was really all right, and after all, school was tomorrow, and we had new red ribbons for our hair.

I wish I could give my sisters delicate flowers, lavender lilacs from the garden, spider webs strewn with diamonds of liquid dew. I would tell them stories, and the night would feel gentle, like the angels around us were nodding. I wanted their days to be soft and green with necklaces of freshwater pearls around their necks. My sisters were believers in my dreams.

I love it when the new moon appears, crescent silver light; the horizon still holds on to the sun's last colors and the blue slowly fades to purples and black in the western sky. New moon nights were our favorite times. My sisters and I always made our wishes on that night. We would sit in the backyard, silent, waiting for the blackness to cover us, and make our wishes. As the new moon always returned, our dreams never strayed too far away.

Mabel Elease is Mama's name. Isn't that pretty? Like organdy or satin dresses, garden paths, peonies, lilacs, real china plates bought one at a time, that was my mama. Lonely were the nights, and black was the sorrow Mama felt on those nights Daddy didn't come home. I'd wake up and she would be pacing in her bedroom, crying softly, cigarette after cigarette to keep her company. Loneliness came to her room again, walked in like he was her best friend. Her room must have looked so bare, all her hopes and dreams were not there.

Seems like everybody else slept through the pain, why not me? Looking through the midnight windowpane, the streets dark and deserted, and the moon a silver crescent, I could feel Mama's pain drift heavily through the house like some unwanted incense. Other families seemed so normal, why did Daddy have to stray? Weren't we enough? The night gave no answers, and sleep was always fitful.

I dreaded the fights when Daddy arrived home in the early morning. By then all the kids were up, and the shouts and blows were like thunder and lightning, like an attack. Oh, brother, get ready for school, comb the girls' hair, fix grits and eggs for breakfast, fix lunches, paint on a smile, and wish there was someone to talk to. When I complained to Grandma, her big frame would droop a little, so I stopped talking too much, 'cause she would just look too sad. Daddy was her only child, and she wished for the best for us.

When Mama came into a room it was like the sunlight entered, first light soft and warm, before the heat of the day begins and you can fry an egg on the sidewalk. On the good days Mama was like a rambling pink wild rose, the kind that sprawls forever. The good days, pound cakes and fried chicken, laughter, company, kids welcome, house open and vibrating with love. We played bid whist games on the front porch, and drank iced tea while the grownups barbecued. The hot summer sun filtered down through the trees, throwing lacy patterns on the table and the grass.

These enchanted moments kept at bay the dark clouds that seemed to always follow the light, like the fog rolls in off the sea after the days get too hot, covering the shoreline with gray drizzle. Sometimes that was Mama; her big bosom spelled comfort, her arms offered security and tenderness, and her ears were open to listen to our silent fears.

Then bad days would enter the house, like some dark gloom, and our slightest mistake would warrant slaps — bed not made up properly, laundry not done, dishes dirty, we played too long. On the bad days, the darkness covered our house, our yard, and our hearts. That was the frightening thing about grownups, the silences, the not explaining, leaving us frightened and resentful.

My sisters and I did the best we could, determined to marry well and never end up like Mama, sad and lonely when Daddy was gone, bright like a new rose when things went well, meaning when Daddy came home regular.

I always knew Daddy loved us — after all, he built us doll houses, a playhouse; he encouraged us, took us fishing and camping, out for Sunday drives with ice cream at the Frosty Freeze. Daddy always insisted we break the cycle of poverty by studying and staying in school. Yeah, he loved us, but then again his own daddy had his legal wife, and Grandma Emma was his woman, so who knows? Who's to say? I think he just loved two women, and that was definitely taboo — or was it? We kids were in the dark without a light.

Chapter 4

Easter Sunday and Joy is In the Air

Easter Sunday was the afternoon to be sitting on Grandma's porch. The lilies were in full bloom and an ancient magnolia tree shaded the front porch. It was a good place to sit. Grandma lived on Davis Avenue, the main drag. Her house was next door to Miss Ossie's beauty shop, which was next door to the barbershop with the red-and-white pole outside. The grocery store across the street was where we could buy ham hocks, neck bones, collard greens, hot sausages, everything on credit.

Easter Sunday was fun, after the long, boring Catholic Mass. The part about Jesus rising from the dead was kind of inspiring, but nobody else we knew rose from the coffin, so I didn't really believe it. The fun for me was watching the younger girls look for the Easter Bunny and hunt for the eggs Bobby and I dyed. There was always ham for dinner. Mama made us frilly Easter dresses of organdy or soft cotton. She crocheted our white cotton hats, then starched and ironed them so the brim stood up, and a big ribbon held it together. We got new patent-leather Mary Jane shoes and new socks. Life was good.

The biggest thrill was watching the ladies parade down Davis Avenue in their new clothes and hats. I swear black women invented hats. Grandma's house was between the Holiness and Methodist churches, so we had a chance to enjoy the parade. The women wore wide-brimmed straw hats bedecked with silk flowers, black silk hats trimmed with velvet, turbans, hats with birds on them, hats that covered one eye, lace hats, netting-over-the-eye hats.

The women were all dressed to the nines in their formfitting shoulder-pad dresses or cute two-piece suits. Most of these clothes were handmade and the very height of fashion. Some of the dresses and hats matched. Oh, me, oh my, there was no end to fashion. They wore gloves, white, cream, black, beige. Their stockings with black lines up the back of their legs were sexy. We girls couldn't wait to grow up and dress fine. Rosy red lips, waved hair, sexy hats, exotic gloves, Easter meant style to me.

The Holiness Church down the street was my favorite. It was just a little white painted building with a huge old chinaberry tree and a couple of sycamores in front for shade. I'd sit there sometimes to hear the singing. Mama was starting to take catechism classes to be baptized a Catholic, and she never wanted me to go there, but I did anyway. I loved the beautiful flapping cloth fans with wooden handles that folded shut. They usually had a picture of Jesus, but sometimes birds were on them, too.

These women smelled sweet like perfume. Their skin was all lotioned down, glossy and smooth, and they could sing! I never wanted to sing in our choir, tired-old Gregorian chants, ancient Ave Marias, hell no! The Holiness people sang in harmony, high crystal-clear voices, lighter than air, deep low voices like the forest. Four hundred years of captivity, four hundred years of faith in deliverance. Yep, sitting outside that little old paint-peeling, color-paned windows building, the preacher sweating, his handkerchief wet from his fervent preaching, a workingman's church.

God visited — our God, the brown one, deep-as-the-night one, protector of souls, harbor in the storm, hater of racism, and lover of justice. Our brown God was there, lover of old black men and women and tender children. I loved that old run-down freedom-singing Holiness Church.

Beautiful May days came, long and languid, humidity rising, wildflowers blooming, flower buds opening, blue-sky days. The green of the earth, the smell of the warming soil, enchanted my young soul. The turquoise sky kissed the land. Every May first, all the Catholic schools marched a couple of miles downtown in honor of the Virgin Mary. We would gather in front of the white folks' cathedral. I called it that secretly, of course, 'cause by that time Mama had been converted, and she looked upon any thoughts criticizing the Church as heresy.

Off to march we went, all dressed in white, all the black kids in the back, of course. We gathered to sing to the blessed pale-faced Virgin who gave not a rat's ass about us, I swear. Yeah, Mama bought it hook, line, and sinker, Jesus, God, Virgin Mary, miracles, guilt, fish on Friday, mortal sins, venial sins, the list went on forever. Mama had me baptized a Catholic. Even though I objected, she insisted, "Cat, you will burn in hell if you reject the truth."

Now that Mama is a born-again Catholic, we have to go to confession on Saturdays. Imagine looking through latticework so woven you can barely see the priest's profile. He's huddled in his box, poor bored man, playing God, listening to grown people and little kids like us confess our sins. Hell, I made up sins when my week had been uneventful, felt sorry for the man, having to sit there for hours. I tried to give him something to forgive. There was always some penance, Hail Marys, the rosary, and the Lord's Prayer, which I never did.

Bobby rode his bike to confession one Saturday afternoon, of all the dumb things to do. He saved money for a year to buy that bright red Schwinn bike. We were so glad for him 'cause he would ride us on the handlebars. While he was confessing his sins, which I doubt if he had anything too hot to tell, some rogue stole his bike. His dream was gone. He hadn't bought a lock. Me, I had only my feet to get around on. I felt bad for Bobby. He was just good, and life dealt him a low blow.

What a great summer day! School is out and freedom is ours. The rain was pouring down, gray, cold, and hard. The streets were running rivers, and of course Betty, Peggy, and I had to walk through the flooded parts, soaking wet, happy, naughty. We knew we weren't supposed to, but the water was so much fun, little currents swirling around us. The sadness was waiting for us when we got home. It felt like some unknown presence was in the house, gloomy. Mama broke the news that Aunt Minnie and Leslie, my buddy, my pal, and my port in the storm of life, were leaving.

Mama was in tears when she told me. Old Bubbah Gaines had done it again — how I hated that man. Another woman, another scandal, and Aunt Minnie had had enough. Since she married Bubbah she'd had three kids in five years. Billy, Jane, and Pat were our little cousins. We used to dress them and hug them, and loved them fiercely.

Aunt Minnie was not so glamorous anymore. She lost the sparkle; the zest and the stars over her fiery red head were gone. She wore a cloak of sadness. The entire town knew Bubbah was no good, so tall and willowy, curly dark hair, eyes like a deep cool river inviting you to jump in. He was the color of chicory coffee, handsome and dangerous, hands of a doctor, heart of stone.

They lived in the upscale part of town, right next door to his parents Mr. Andrew and Miss Theresa. They were devout Methodists, cold and proud, richer than a lot of white people. They never liked Aunt Minnie or us. They said we had no class. I always hated to visit there; that big old brick house looked unlived in. Their fine furniture was like you weren't supposed to sit on it. Oh, brother, give me a shack and a good-old fig tree.

There we all are, Mama crying, all us girls sad. The lights in the living room are dim as the shades are drawn against the heat of the day. It's unnaturally quiet in the house. Their suitcases are packed and they're leaving, headed to some faraway town.

We never knew how hard Aunt Minnie's heart was grieving, and Mama says somehow she feels like she let her down. My cousin Leslie is leaving me. This old town can be so lonely, late at night the wind blows cold, and the loneliness makes you shiver. Leslie, my keeper of secrets, my cousin, is leaving me.

Part of me hurt so bad inside I wanted to walk down to the little creek and just sit and sit and wonder why the things we love so much have to vanish. Mr. Bubbah was an important, rich black doctor, so of course, as the laws of Alabama ran, he was given full custody of our cousins. Poor Aunt Minnie moved down here to be with Mama and us, and now she is leaving without her babies. This wasn't Chicago, and the laws were different. Money ruled. Aunt Minnie, redheaded darling, bearer of dreams, teller of stories, spunky, truth-talking, was broken.

Aunt Minnie and Leslie went to Chicago where Aunt Minnie had a friend to take them in. We were all silent in the living room, Mama, my sisters, and me. Bobby was just moping around outside. I was thinking 'bout my own Mama, bruised some, slapped some, cheated on, and still she stayed. Thank you, angel, 'cause we would have nowhere to go. We just sat there till the light faded slowly from the sky and the distant sound of the train could be heard. Fly away home, my cousin, fly away home

I swear I moped around all sour and grumpy, shoes untied, hair nappy, books scattered on the floor. Months went by with me missing Leslie. No more Saturday sleepovers or gossiping the way only first cousins can. We had so many racing contests, and loved flirting with the cute boys, all those moments gone. Leslie began to write me, bless her heart, and the world became light again.

What a lovely day, a letter addressed to me all the way from Chicago. I smell the envelope to try to get an idea of the big city. Quickly I go to my room, lie on my bed, and feel her all around me, bright eyes looking into mine, soft little soul telling me of her joys and sorrows.

These letters were a link, a trail, a path, and traces of my cousin. I'd write back quickly, tell her jokes, gossip, and reassure her when we got older we would live in New York, Harlem or Greenwich Village, be poets, painters, singers, wear high-style clothes and be beautiful. *Ebony* magazine always showed famous black people who lived in New York, so that was our plan.

So many hot summer afternoons I'd get into trouble for getting home too late to help with dinner, laundry, or some other monotonous chore. I always — I mean a lot — went down by the swamp, past the dump, to visit some new kids I had met. So funny, the forbidden land was about two miles past our house, where the road ended and the dump was located. Lo and behold, past the stinky old dump was a narrow red clay trail leading past the swampy area. We were definitely forbidden to go there, I'm talking on pain of a beating. The exciting, scary rumors of crocodiles, snakes, and poisonous scorpions kept us champing at the bit. Hell, we wanted to go there!

There were people who lived in little shacks on government land, close to the woods, something I'd never known, and I loved it. Little board shacks at the end of the trail, zinc roofs and a porch if you're rich, poverty to some, fun to me.

Many cotton pickers and farm laborers lived here and survived between jobs. There was cooking outside, rocks formed in a circle with a grill on top, pots boiling or meat sizzling, wild game, catfish, beans, rice, collard greens, sweet potatoes cooked in their skins. It felt so good to be around the women cooking over an open fire. The air was filled with the sounds of babies crying, women laughing, everybody doing a little bit.

My friend Parnell and his four sisters lived here. I fell in love with them. Four girls to a bed, Parnell, his sisters, and their parents were all in one room, sheets hung neat and clean on bamboo rods to give each bed area a little privacy. Miss Paulette, Parnell's mama, was dark and dimpled, and she could cook and laugh while hugging me like I was one of her own. They had the least but gave the most. Mama would be waiting for me when I would get home too late, her eyes all wide and angry. "You been down to the dump again, where those no-account people live, trash people."

"Common Negroes," my Mama would say. I would look down at my run-down scuffed shoes, tattered play clothes, knee skinned from running too hard, and hair as wild as un-mown grass. Common? Of course. Daisies, dandelions, chicory, sweet peas, goldenrod waving, wildflowers standing by the railroad tracks, unruly flowers, untamed people, were common.

Miss Frazier wasn't common. She had a pretty white painted house, fancy to us, with big hydrangeas and azaleas by the front porch. Miss Frazier was yellow skinned, tall, and knobby looking; skinny as a rail, eyes flat, all elbows and knees. Her tight lips were pressed together firmly, lest some soft word escape. She was always telling us to not pick her flowers. Well, if she was Mama's model, I was doomed. "Common Negroes," Mama would say, and my breath would become still. The clouds were looking down on me, smiling, to keep me calm. Mama was so wrong, so wrong to judge hearts by what material things they owned.

Of course I loved the common people Mama looked down upon. I loved that family. The kids were all wild-haired, cussing bad words, chasing bullfrogs, smoking some, and stealing watermelons. They really seemed like the gypsies I read about. Eating cornbread and beans was a fine meal 'cause I was there and they shared what they had.

Little board shack at the end of the road, what good times we had there, take it easy, the road's full of holes, how I ran to be near them. This family was mine, not too many secrets here, what you see is what you get, relaxed, poor, singing, laughing, sighing, crying, on the edge of the swamp.

I don't really know too much about Grandma Emma's past. She was tall, and I know for a fact on gambling nights she carried a small pistol in her right-hand apron pocket. I know that Grandma was my port in every storm and did her best to protect me from the wrath of my parents. My grandma was taller then most men, and bigger too, so to me she was invincible. I always knew she would protect me if she could, 'cause I was way too young to know that life was full of light and rain.

I felt a sudden chill one stormy winter day; the rain was falling outside the window, and Grandma's face was shadowed and slightly transparent, like she could fade away and I couldn't hold on to her. I started bawling because I felt the fear of losing her. My grandma was bigger than life, the keeper of my heart, her eyes dark and soft, letting me walk in. Her hands were never so busy that she wouldn't take time to hold me close to her sweet-smelling bosom.

That fear of losing her surfaced like the bogeyman we kids were scared of at night. I guess I realized Grandma was only human; even though she looked like she could sail on the wind, ride wild horses, and defend herself against all kinds of evil, she was human, just like me.

All the angels seemed to stay around that sacred scene, just my grandma and me. No words, just the knowledge that the world my mama brought me to was way too big, and I was small, and without my grandma was their any help at all? Is there any justice at all? The only thing that drowned my sorrow was Grandma's big soft lap and a cold soda pop.

The days are short now; winter has set in, and the sun hangs low in the sky. Winter, the season of the darkening of the light, the time when we are forced to go within. As the earth lies dormant, the trees stripped of their leaves, and the flowers sleeping, we too are in our still time. Thankfully, Christmas is near, that magical time of lights hung on trees, bright-colored ribbons, presents, and the awesome expectation of a miracle.

Christmas was festive, with relatives visiting, and plenty of food and whiskey. The songs of Billie Holiday and Nat King Cole serenaded us on those warm party nights. There were hushed voices as we were forced to go to sleep listening to laughter and the tinkle of ice in the kitchen. The warm smells of turkey, gravy, and pies promised a feast ahead. Christmas to a small child was fairy land; the angel hair on the tree, itchy stuff, but beautiful, twinkling lights, good food, Santa Claus, and presents.

As we got older the rhythm changed. I remember telling my little sisters there was no Santa Claus, mean old me. They, of course, cried as I smirked. What a brat! I found our presents hidden way back in Mama's closet. I was as usual snooping around where I had no business, so my sisters, after the initial shock of no Mr. Claus, joined me in carefully opening all our presents and then re-wrapping them. On Christmas morning we were blasé as hell. This marked the beginning of growing up, the ending of fairy tales, golden sails, and comic book heroes.

As we got older the responsibility of Christmas fell on Bobby and me, to help load the tree with decorations, and make sure the smaller ones had homemade Christmas presents. Bobby, Betty, and I were the oldest, and as our responsibilities grew, so did the love. We embroidered handkerchiefs and pillowcases, and made homemade pillows and sachets stuffed with rose petals and lavender. Daddy and Bobby hand carved wooden toy cars for Tony. Betty helped dress the young ones, and love was the light that warmed us when it felt like our own little world was exploding.

One December, when Mama and Daddy had one of their famous fights, Daddy left and Mama went to her room. Bobby, bless his young boy heart, helped Betty and me get the tree, decorate it, and buy and wrap presents for the young ones. We did Christmas that year — cooked the dinner, and acted as if the world were still full of angels, bright stars, and rainbows. The looks of wonder on their little faces made it the best season in our childhood. Giving, not receiving, the love we gave came back a thousand times.

Whenever we made our visits to Aunt Hattie's in Memphis, I loved her church. At that old church I always felt God and the devil had a truce. The sinners and the saints, the killer and the monk, the whore and the preacher's wife, all were invited there. The voices of those women singing lifted my soul to the rim of the sky, and pushed me through to the place where dreams were made. My Christmas had not much to do with the little white Jesus and his virgin mother.

No, my God lived like us, was brown, and had more than his share of hard knocks, but responded with childlike kindness. My Jesus was never hung on a cross, lynched maybe. My brown Jesus would never pass the shanty houses down by the dump and not leave the little children their warm clothes and dollies and toy trucks.

My hero, Jesus, would never let my Mama cry down in the laundry room when she was just too tired to finish the mountain of clothes that had to be done for her to be paid. No, he would touch all the mean people's hearts, and open their eyes to the beauty of early rose sunrises and children's first cries in the morning. I never told my mama any thoughts like this. I only told my grandma. She would look at me funny and declare; "Cat, you sure were born a strange one." But then again, so was she.

On one of our Sunday drives with Daddy, we drove way deep into the country. We were driving by the water. Daddy was looking for a good place to fish and for us to have a picnic. There was a crowd of black people by the side of the road, and Daddy pulled over to let us see a country baptism. The preacher and the saved ones stood knee-deep in the clear Alabama water. All dressed in white, the congregation sang as the saved ones were dipped into the water of forgiveness. They sang with bursting hearts, these old black and brown people. Forgiveness was etched on their old and sometimes young faces.

I was so lucky to have a big family; there were six of us. Bobby was my oldest brother. I swear he looked like an Arab I saw in our geography book. He had olive skin, a hawk nose, almond eyes, and an African stature. My brother was honest and kind, never known to lie. I, on the other hand, was pretty much a ne'er-do-well.

I would go up to white people on the street, pretend I was lost, and get money from them, then gleefully buy bags of candy. Or I would walk miles into fancy white neighborhoods, go to the back door, tell the maid I was lost, and get bus fare and food. I was bad, but also curious. I wanted to look into those big houses, see behind the veil, the wall, meet white kids, see what was so different. Not my brother. Oh, no, Bobby was the good one, an altar boy, for Christ's sake.

While my sisters and I were busy ditching church and spending the collection money on donuts and soda, Bobby would be serving God. Yes, he was honest, or dishonest, couldn't quite figure it out. He would blackmail us, smirking like a cat who has the poor little mouse cornered. Give him candy or he would tell Mama we skipped church. Oh, brother! But he was kind, and saved me from many a licking I would have gotten from having such a big mouth. As we got older, my brother had a newspaper route, and many a time he would treat to the movies with his earnings.

After me came Miss Betty Jo, tall at birth like Grandma's side of the family, brown, regal, full of mouth, and slender of build. Betty was determined, and not as much of a troublemaker as I was, but she could be persuaded now and again to participate in illegal things like our gambling operations. Betty somehow managed not to get beat as much as I did. She was far too levelheaded — her brown eyes and sweet smile would keep even Lucifer at bay. She could pour on the charm when it became necessary.

My sister Peggy was my favorite. Small in stature; her skin was light brown velvet. Peggy was always so gentle. I remember her, eyes shining, hair fuzzy and soft around her heart-shaped face, waiting for us to return home from school. There she would be, all smiles 'cause we were there. And the day would be better.

What was it Peggy and I shared? What twist of fate was in store for us? Her lips were soft and her heart was in her eyes. I always wanted to protect Peggy. She was never a fighter. I was not one to run from a battle, and probably started enough in my day, but Peggy was different, the fragile one.

Linda, my next sister, was born yellow skinned with the nappiest yellow hair in the state of Alabama. Holy cow! She looked like someone had shocked her and her hair just frizzed out, permanently. But she was a little dimpled darling, hazel-green eyes, big, full African mouth, big old African booty, what a girl, and the littlest troublemaker. We petted and spoiled her and worried, as Mama's wrath grew more fearsome after each child was born. Then along came Tony, with his coffee-brown skin, dark, nappy hair, walnut-brown eyes, and a sweet dimpled body. He was the baby boy of the brood.

I finally realized that Grandma Emma's illegal gambling house was a source of much-needed money. The older we grew, the more demands there were for money. I needed money, and cleaning up after the games was a source of quick cash. Grandma's cleaning job helped me buy cloth to sew clothes, socks, barrettes, ribbons, comic books, dime-store jewelry — all the things we couldn't afford.

I was too naïve to wonder who the pretty brown and ebony women were who stayed in the back rooms when the games were going. All I knew was they were so beautiful, with their red lips and smooth young bodies. How I envied them. Secrets, secrets.

My sisters and I were definitely cut from some different cloth than my brother. When we got older, we decided to be like Grandma Emma and have poker parties on Saturday afternoons. This was done secretly, of course, under the big sycamore tree way in the back of the yard, behind the chicken house. This got to be a popular sport, and kids would work all week and come to our backyard to gamble. Things were going on swell.

My sisters and I started selling lemonade and sandwiches, all innocent-like till some uptight neighbor called the cops and we were raided. Yep, end of story. Mama was furious, and told Daddy, "These children are imitating your mama." Daddy for once wasn't too angry with us. He gambled for extra money. He warned us about the police coming to our yard and said, "Grandma can go to jail for her poker games, and you are definitely too young to gamble. Please don't bring trouble." We tried to look innocent and sorrowful, but we still continued to play poker, we were just more secretive.

Chapter 5

Life Gets Stranger By the Minute

Eleven years old, and you bet your bottom dollar life ain't no bed of roses. School must be my punishment for being curious and asking too many questions. The more I read, the more I want to know, want somebody to explain to me why my mama and daddy have to struggle so much. Why does the color of our skin determine our worth? These questions got me into too much trouble with the teachers, so I learned to just shut up. Our classroom has so many different kinds of kids: take Eunice for example. She seems to be angry a lot, and likes to pick on me and call me "ugly girl." Marcella sits next to me, and is so shy she hardly talks to any of us in class. Charlotte has a knack for making jokes and staying in trouble with the nuns.

I just want to be pretty like Evelyn. I swear she looks just like a young princess walking through a palace. So pretty, her skin dark brown satin, cheeks high, eyes so dark the night sky resembles them, and her body is light and curvy. She always smells like lotion and sweet flowers. Hell, here I am, trying my best to look elegant like her, and I don't stand a chance. My hair won't stay shiny and black, pressed smooth like hers. My frizzy mop stands around my face like some kind of brown cotton candy, and this yellow-brown skin definitely ain't in. Oh, well, at least I can play baseball, fly a kite high as any boy, and marbles is still my game, but deep inside, beauty is my aim, glamour my plan. The boys in school look cuter by the minute, and the art of flirting is exciting.

We are still living on St. Ann's street; thank the Lord. That old, sprawling oak tree in the backyard is still my savior. Nobody's developed behind us, so the woods and our sweet creek remain. Every day the town grows, and some of the back roads are soon to be paved. Progress, yeah, still tense old Alabama, lynchings on the back roads, blacks and Indians being jailed for the littlest things, no money. Good-old Alabama — the truth is starting to grow through the sidewalk cracks.

Aunt Hattie and Uncle T.C. were always part of our lives. Aunt Hattie raised her sister's children, Mama especially, after the other two were taken north. For two weeks every summer, Bobby, my sisters, and I got to stay with them in Memphis. Uncle T.C. smelled of gin, quinine water, and after-shave lotion. He was short, slender, and the color of pecans, a card player and dice roller, reckless. He was good to us, and his laughter rang through the house. Aunt Hattie was as round as she was tall, chocolate brown, all dimples, laugh lines crinkly around her eyes and mouth.

Our job was to work with Aunt Hattie in the mornings in the big house. She and Uncle T.C. lived in the worker's cabin way in the back of the yard, where the fig trees and gardens were. We had to learn the fine trade of polishing silver and furniture, ironing clothes properly, scrubbing floors on our hands and knees, and to always look down when talking to white people, and say yes sir and yes ma'am. Oh, brother!

The great reward was when we got to go play afternoons at Miss Pearlie's house. She was Uncle T.C.'s sister. They lived in a run-down black neighborhood. Juke joints and fried chicken restaurants were on the main street. There were kids all through the area, so the fun was endless. We girls played hopscotch and jacks, and sang songs to the radio. The boys played marbles, me right along with them. Hot afternoons we would laze around playing Monopoly or card games.

Memphis was famous for music, and we were thrilled to see real musicians, with their conked hair, driving big Buicks. There were beauty salons where we could smell the burnt hair and see the beautiful women come out, hair all pressed, their lips red and sexy. The men with their fancy suits and sleek women so impressed me. Music literally floated through the hot Tennessee air. I, the country mouse, was enchanted with the noise and excitement. Yet oppression littered the streets. We were second-class citizens in Tennessee, the home of the Ku Klux Klan,

The old folks say that when the rain falls and the sun shines, the devil's beating his wife, and when the red-tailed hawk circles overhead we're in for fair weather. Summer is full of surprises, one day the air fragrant and sweet as a baby's breath, later the same day the heavens split open and drench the earth. The storm clouds gather, hanging low, the sky hazy and gray, and then the rumblings of thunder are heard way in the distance.

We kids all stopped playing and scattered for home. First we would gather in the kitchen, unplug all the electrical appliances, close the windows, and open the curtains so we could see the marvel. The thunder got louder and angrier sounding, and the air became still, tense, and yellow. The thunder came nearer, and the house seemed to shake. The lightning struck, violent white forks, but I swear, when tornadoes were near, or a hurricane approached, those lightning shafts would be red-gold or blue-green, scary.

We counted the seconds in between the thunderclaps so we could figure how close the lightning was. Believe me, many times the electrical energy materialized and floated in space, eerie. Lightning raced through the fields, through streets, striking trees at random, and occasionally killing anyone unlucky enough to be too close to a tree. The wrath of Mother Earth was energy uncontrolled. Tornadoes happened mostly north of us, but sometimes the devil funnel swept through south Alabama ripping roofs, trailers, churches, you name it. Grandma said, "Cat, I swear that's probably why folks here are so ignorant — all that electricity fried their brains."

Oh, the glory of thunder and lightning storms. We would look out the window and quake with fear as the lightning raced across the farmlands. There were dreadful stories of neighbors electrocuted in the streets. In Alabama, even the storms were bigger than life.

The darkness of the hot summer nights seemed to make brilliant stars fall at my door, made the wind sing and howl, made the day violent with wind and storms. The trees bowed to the wind, and the old oaks groaned, some of them falling violently to the ground, their massive shallow roots torn out of the wet earth.

Hurricanes were different. When the radio gave out warnings, we hunkered down. The winds battered our little board houses, and sometimes a roof was blown off, windows popped out, houses flattened. Nature at work was the real thing. We kids loved and feared it. Hurricane season in Alabama was terrifying. The light would become sulfur yellow, and the air would be deathly still. Everyone hurried to their homes, for we knew too well the danger of the earth when she was aroused.

Some of our friends, the Woods boys, Lonnie and Albert, lived around the corner from us on a dirt road leading off the main paved Montgomery Avenue. They lived in an old, rambling brown board house, with a wraparound porch and lots of flowers. Lonnie was my age and a natural prankster. We were born the same year, but boy, he was light years ahead of me. He was a good-looking kid, brown eyes so dark they bordered on black, tan-brown skin, and the curly black hair he'd inherited from his mama.

Lonnie was fun, his mouth almost always turned up with mischief, and his eyes could shine. His brother Albert was seven years older. Lonnie feared and loved him. Lonnie was younger so Albert ruled, firm. Hell, he'd smack Lonnie for any silly thing. Of course, his younger brother — bee in his bonnet, pest in his domain — raided his room regularly, rifled through all of Albert's personal stuff, blew up his cherry bombs, stole his precious comic books. When he was ten, Lonnie stole Albert's coin collection — I'm talking *all* the coins. Was he brave or stupid? We couldn't figure it out, but it was fun when Lonnie spent all those valuable coins for ice-cream sodas, hot dogs, comics, balloons, you name it. We partied till every dime was gone, to hell with the consequences!

Lonnie and I had this in common: trouble was our middle name. Yikes! Albert was big enough to kill Lonnie, but he didn't, just a lot of cuffs and threats. Albert would let Lonnie tie him up when they played cowboys. Then, when Lonnie untied him, Albert, being as he had some bone to pick with Lonnie, would tie Lonnie up after their parents went to work, and leave him tied all day till just before Miss Beatrice came home from work. Just one of many tortures he inflicted upon Lonnie, not that Lonnie didn't ask for it.

Boy, Lonnie was brave. He once had the gall to empty his brother's yellow mouthwash down the sink, then piss in the bottle. The wash looked yellow, so Albert didn't suspect a thing, and he took a big swig. Lonnie was tortured again. He couldn't help himself. His older brother was his mountain to conquer, his foe, and his best friend. Albert, tall, slim, fair, and definitely a calculating athletic kid, was an achiever. Well, he got so tired of Lonnie raiding his room, he bought a shrunken head from the traveling black carnival. That head was terrible, real, I reckoned, mouth and eyes sewn shut, black matted hair, eerie to a kid, bloodcurdling.

Albert hung this head in his window. He then had the nerve to hand sew a white voodoo doll, black embroidery thread eyes and nose, with the mouth sewn shut. Albert was desperate; his nimble fingers were anxious to keep Lonnie from his treasures, so forces of nature come on in. Lonnie always broke Albert's stuff, so it was a two-way street. Still, Albert's stuff was fun, bow and real arrows, BB gun, tons of marbles, games, Frankenstein model, erector set — hell, we all were awed at that museum of a room. I think Albert kept everything he ever had.

That voodoo doll sat on the shelf, with pins stuck at random all over its body, especially the six-inch-long needle with an eight ball on the end of it. Albert told Lonnie if he ever touched his stuff again the needle would go into the doll's heart and he would die. We snuck into Albert's room and Lonnie showed me. I almost died of fright as we bolted from the terrible scene. End of Lonnie's rummaging where he didn't belong.

This nightmare of the voodoo doll went on for months. Boredom for Lonnie, because rifling Albert's room was fun and it seemed to be Lonnie's only way of getting even with his big brother. Well, Miss Beatrice decided to spring clean Albert's room — you know that time of the year when all the mamas go mad, gleam in their eye, housedresses on, aprons tied tightly, dust-mop in hand, rugs taken out, draped over the clothesline and beat with a broom. This was usually our job. We hated spring-cleaning; leave well enough alone was our motto.

Miss Beatrice spied that shrunken head and that stuffed voodoo doll and had a royal fit. She was a devout Methodist, and had no truck with outdated African magic. She put the head and the doll with the pins in a box to burn them. Lonnie called me over, and Miss Beatrice said I could watch Jesus burn that evil box. I wouldn't have missed it for all the diamonds in Africa. Free at last, Lonnie would be rid of that awful spell. Miss Beatrice was big, kind of fat, but muscular; no man in his right mind would ever pick a fight with her.

Miss Beatrice sang in the choir, and was known to be a genuine Bible thumper, She had us hold hands while she sang and begged Jesus to burn that box and banish the evil spirits. We waited and waited. It was getting harder and harder not to laugh, and squirming was the only thing I could do. Finally, as the sun seemed to relinquish its hot chokehold on the June afternoon, Miss Beatrice gave up, lit a fire with matches, and burned the box. We were glad the threat was gone. Of course, Miss Beatrice gave Albert a lock for his door, and Lonnie was banished forever to just being little brother.

Lamar lived in the fanciest house in our part of town. His family's front yard was big enough for four houses, and their home was fine enough for the mayor to live in. We loved to visit Lamar. His mama, Miss Gloria, was so good to us. She had a maid, and was high in society, but that didn't make me feel shy around her. Miss Gloria had a warm smile, and her Louisiana accent was soft. "Cat, how you doing? How's your mama and daddy? Come on in, and make yourself at home. Lamar will be right down."

Their house was light and spacious. Big windows lit their living room, with its soft gray wool carpets and chairs big enough to sleep on. We mostly sat around the kitchen table where the maid, Miss Lola, gave us sandwiches and drinks. Lamar's room was full of books and toys, and we spent hours playing there. He was the only kid with a television, and since he was an only child, he was happy to have us around. Lamar was one of my best friends when I was in my tomboy phase. Of course he had every toy known to childhood, and was generous in sharing.

Lamar's daddy, Mr. Williams, was well known around town, and important in civil rights issues. He held meetings at his house, and was trying to force St. Bernard's, the white Catholic school, to enroll Lamar. He was starting the process of opening the door to integrating the schools in Mobile.

Mr. Williams was so respected that we were all shocked when the news spread that he had killed himself. He was the wealthiest black man in our town; he owned two funeral homes and a big house, and had a fine Creole wife. Miss Gloria was the delicate, bronze, wavy-haired lady who always put fresh flowers on the altar, and changed the linens in the church. Mr. Williams should never have killed himself — hell, he had two Cadillacs and a maid.

One dark night as the winds howled and wailed, the dark-of-the-moon time, when voices seemed to be talking through time, Mr. Williams stood in the living room. Illuminated by a floor lamp in the corner, he raised a pistol to his head and shot himself. Little could he know in his forsaken soul that Lamar was in the hallway. Scared of the winds, he'd come looking for comfort.

So that boy child of eleven years, richest black boy in town, met death head-on, and the joy in him faded, distant, his youth already spent. Nothing we could say on that gray-ass, bleak, January day. No hope for the sun to break through the sullen clouds, the earth deep green and winter brown. This life gets hard to understand when you're still a boy and not a man.

I wished I were a magician. I would part the sky for him, do anything to stop the sadness. Wished I had a secret stairway to the stars, or clouds for us to sit on way above human sorrow, but I could only hold his hand, 'cause we were way too young to understand.

After Mr. Williams was buried you would think things would get back to normal for Lamar and Miss Gloria. She was so pretty; she had what we called good hair — naturally straight, with little curls softly hanging around her velvet skin. Don't ever forget she came from New Orleans, home of voodoo. Seems Mr. Williams didn't just die and go to Heaven, oh, no, not in Alabama, the home of ghosts and visions. His friends repeatedly saw him. He always appeared to be scared and unhappy. It got so bad Miss Gloria was afraid to sleep; he would visit her in her dreams, and Lamar was sure he would see his father in different parts of the house, always trying to hang on to him, always crying.

Well, things got so out of hand that Miss Gloria, soft, flower-like Creole lady that she was, went back home to New Orleans, that home of magic and charms from Africa, and brought back a spiritual lady to help Mr. Williams leave this earth.

The healer lady had on a red scarf with bird feathers and a loose-fitting long yellow dress. She never saw us or looked our way, but we saw her, oh yeah, tall, yellow skin, with eyes that seemed to look through space and time. There were bowls of water in the yard being purified. We were forbidden to go to Lamar's house for the ceremony. Mama said it was a sacrilege to God. But Conrad, Charlotte, Portia, and I did go. We sat in the backyard, hidden behind the azalea bushes. We were close enough to the back porch to hear and see the drumming and singing. The ceremony was on the red cement floor on the patio, which the spiritual lady covered with all kinds of symbols in chalk — weird, fun.

We could see the candles burning, smell the incense, hear the obeah lady singing, twisting, and doing some strange trance dance. She had a young drummer with her. He was short, and dark as night, and seemed to have coal-burning eyes. A scarf was tied around his head, and bird feathers fitted over his left ear. We loved him. A big drum hung from a red woven strap over his shoulder. Looking neither right or left, he kept up a steady rhythm as the healer danced. Felt like Africa was in the yard.

Maybe it was the wind, the moon, the stillness around the house, but we indeed felt Mr. Williams's spirit rush into the heavens like a mighty gust of wind. I swear Heaven spread her arms and embraced his newly freed soul. He was let go, and Miss Gloria and Lamar were rid of some dark burden. We all got goose bumps, and I wanted to slip through that green pathway, back to the safety of what I could see. Enough for one day of exploring life and death and the powers that lay way beyond my grasp — I just wanted to run home.

Charlotte was never too afraid. She would always climb the highest tree, run the fastest, and jump the highest when we played jump rope. Charlotte, Betty, and I decided to become professional poker players, gamblers. Charlotte's mama, Miss Louise, gambled at Grandma's on

Saturday nights, so Charlotte knew poker like we did. We bought cards, and saved our pennies and change in Mason jars, always ready to play. Mama forbade us to gamble for money, but we still did. She loved to say, "A liar will surely burn in hell, and God sees every bad thing you do."

Boy, the night the house caught on fire, I remembered Mama's warning and was terrified. We disobeyed her orders and the bedroom was on fire. There we were in our drafty living room, Bobby, Betty, Peggy, Charlotte, Sunny, and I. We thought Linda and Tony were sleeping in their room, all secure and clean. Tony's diapers were changed, and he was happy and asleep — most importantly, asleep.

Soon as Mama and Daddy left to go play bid whist, their favorite card game, at Miss Leona's and Mr. Dickey's house, we immediately — I'm talking seconds after they left that driveway — pulled out the card table and began to gamble. By now we had addicted half the neighborhood to wasting hard-earned money at our house, always done secretly, of course.

So there you have us, Bobby, my obnoxious older brother had by now been hooked on poker. Hell, he even wore a sun visor to look like a pro, the baron we called him, the serious gambler. There we were, folks gone, friends around, Kool-Aid, peanuts, pennies, nickels, dimes, quarters, the Platters singing on the black radio station, "Oh, oh, oh, yes, I'm the great pretender," bliss, warm, crickets, firefly night, all is well.

All of a sudden Linda, the yellow-haired four-year-old, who was supposed to be sleeping, kept running past with glasses of water, running, not saying a word. Where there's smoke, there's fire. We smelled the smoke. We followed her, and sure as hell her bed was aflame, and the curtains by little Tony's bed were flaming madly, fanned by the evening breeze.

We finally put out the fire, comforted the young ones, put away all the gambling evidence, and waited till Mama and Daddy came home. Man, the look on their faces! For the first time I can remember, they didn't whip us. Their relief far outweighed their anger. And we lived to be bad another day. We made up some cockamamie story about how we were so busy reading and listening to the radio we didn't hear a thing. Mama hugged us, and thanked us for saving the rental house.

Linda had been playing with matches and was the culprit. Oh, brother, Linda was only four, and we were to blame.

Mama's sewing business began to thrive, so she hired Miss Lena to sew with her, along with Miss Beatrice. Those ladies were busy! Miss Lena's body was tall and sturdy, and she had serious-looking eyes. She braided her long, thick hair, and it hung way down her back, almost to her waist. She was loud, and had opinions on just about everything. "Cat, she'd say, "follow your dreams, don't let anybody stop you. You are a good girl, and will make your Mama proud."

I was getting into trouble almost daily. I threw a baseball and broke the bedroom window, and was starting to skip school. I would forge Mama's name on notes when I played hooky — just plain tell a lie. School was confusing me with its religious teaching and too much homework. Portia and I were caught stealing rings and bracelets from the dime store. I needed Miss Lena's encouragement.

I knew I was good. Hell, my heart would break daily if I let it. Already poverty and hopelessness made me feel sadness young kids shouldn't have to feel. Miss Lena always made me feel better, because getting into so much trouble was becoming a drag, and I knew I had to change and start controlling my impulses.

I wondered why Miss Lena had such a crazy baby, so weak he couldn't ever sit up, and his eyes just sort of rolled around, and he drooled, too. Of course, all the neighborhood mamas clucked like hens when Mr. Davis left Miss Lena, almost like he blamed her for the baby being born somehow wrong. Leon was almost three years old before he learned to stand alone and reluctantly started to walk, like a wobble-headed little windup toy. He was a darling baby to us, so good-looking, curly black hair, dark brown skin, eyes so black you could look into them forever.

Miss Lena loved that crazy old boy. He would slur when he talked. His eyes often looked heavenward, his ears heard things only babies and animals hear, like his thoughts were forever rearranging themselves. We loved Leon as only kids can. He was like all of ours, our own special baby doll. Miss Lena was Mama's friend and sewing partner. On the days she worked, it was our job to make sure Leon didn't hurt himself. God help anybody who laughed at him, they were in for a big surprise. We defended him and tried to never let the mean kids hurt him. Leon was ten when he learned to tie his shoes, and he had a hard time talking clearly, but we didn't care. We managed to understand him. There were no special schools, so he lived with his mama, grandma, and grandpa.

That's just the way Leon was, forever young. He would dream away hours sitting on their tree-shaded porch. We would visit him at his house when it was too hot to play in the sun. Miss Lena always gave us cookies and ice-cold Kool-Aid, so we were quite content to laze away the hours with Leon. What kind of visions danced through that head? He would be with us and then he would drift away to that special place, that place where we were when we were very young. But we grew up and he didn't.

Every summer we all went back to Canton, Mississippi, fearful to us kids, old Mississippi. There was not one gas station that had a toilet for coloreds, and few colored fountains to even get a drink from. The farther from Alabama we drove, the more scared we became. Alabama was Klan heaven, but we didn't live deep in the country, so it felt safer. Entering Mississippi was strange, more police on the road, rednecked and weird looking. We were always pulled over, and the cops all asked the same damn thing, "Where you headed, boy?" It was hard to find a colored restaurant to eat at. It was pure in-your-face segregation, Confederate flags flying freely, good-old Mississippi.

Grandma's oldest sister was called Aunt Duck, and boy, did we laugh at her name — behind her back, of course. We laughed so hard our sides would hurt and tears would roll. Aunt Duck was a tall woman, with red-brown skin and nut-brown eyes, all kind and squinty from years of working in the hot sun. She always had two long, thick, sunbleached red braids hanging down her back. Her gnarly hands were strong from years of farm work. She and her husband, Uncle Clyde, had a mule and cart in the backyard. They grew cotton and corn, and lived off the land as much as they could. Uncle Clyde hunted a lot, and the bass fishing was excellent. They had chickens and a pig, so they were pretty well off for country folks.

Uncle Clyde was a great man. He sang in their church choir, and was well known all over the county. He had two shotguns in his house, which was a shock to us. What kind of danger was he telling Daddy about? They would talk quietly when we came around, but the air felt scary. Uncle Clyde and Aunt Duck were raising their grandkids, Leroy and Amos, 'cause Don, their only son, and his wife were working in Detroit and sending money home to raise the two boys. Uncle Clyde's overalls were always sweaty and stained, and his straw hat totally fitted his big black head. He was bigger than Aunt Duck, a strapping, handsome, singing country man. He was not mean, but his eyes seemed to say, *don't mess with me.*

Our country cousins introduced us to gorging ourselves on watermelons grown in their garden. We caught crayfish in ditches, and fished for catfish. We even ate possum soup, not my favorite, but that was Canton, Mississippi, for you. My relatives lived on the outskirts of town, where the Klansmen rode freely, and *boy* and *nigger* were common names, no thanks. Aunt Duck and Clyde's wallpaper was made from old catalog pictures, *Ebony* magazine prints, and newspapers. I felt so sophisticated, like a city girl. We were like a novelty, straight from Mobile, in a car, no less. They had an outhouse, and the back grounds had a fence for their mule and horse. Our cousins were near in age to us, so we began poker games, cussing contests, spitting contests, races, whistling, and jumping rope.

The fun thing for me was the church service down the green delta dirt road, lined with magnolias, poplars, pecans, and oaks draped with Spanish moss. All of a sudden we came around a bend and approached this ragged, old, leaning-to-the-side church. The Sunday service was loaded with people. A church full of black and brown women in their fancy hats, some like birds of paradise, others polka dotted and velvet trimmed, some black velvet with gorgeous netting over sexy dark eyes. The women who got the spirit lost their hats a lot 'cause they would fly off when the women went into fits. It looked so funny we'd have to hold down our heads not to laugh.

The women were gorgeous with their Evening-in-Paris smell and their Sunday dresses on. Their fans flapped furiously as the preaching got more intense and the hot air in the old church began to circulate. The men reeked of Old Spice after-shave, and oftentimes moonshine from last night's dice game.

My grandma and daddy always had to sit up front in church and be blessed by the preacher, afterward swarmed by relatives and long-ago friends. We dreaded this trip. Mississippi was so evil we couldn't even play hide-and-go-seek late at night like we did at home. The senseless reaction to civil rights demands only increased the violence and hate. I could sometimes taste the hatred coming from people. Canton, Mississippi, was always the vacation to hell.

Grandma Emma had one baby brother, our Uncle Roscoe. How we loved the man, hands down our favorite relative. He moved to Los Angeles, unbelievable to me, seventeen years young, only five dollars to his name, a paper bag full of clothes, and a bus ticket bought with his cotton-picking wages. My true hero, Uncle Roscoe, gentle as a summer breeze, soft as the robin's song. My sweet uncle was a sissy — that's what they called men who loved men back then. Nobody seemed too put out about it, that's just the way it was. Uncle Roscoe wore glasses, and was of slender build, tall like Grandma, copper colored, with kind brown eyes. Hell, he was the only grownup who even knew us up close. He played Monopoly with us, or poker, pushed us on our swings, listened to our silly songs, and laughed at our jokes. My, oh my, we loved him.

Like hundreds of other young black men in the delta, Uncle Roscoe migrated west after reading the handbills advertising for laborers in California's farmlands. Grandma's lady friend, Miss Gladys, answered an ad for domestic work in Los Angeles, and she left Mississippi, too. Hell, seemed like half the South was migrating, everybody, that is, except Daddy. Uncle Roscoe moved on up from being a farm laborer to a chef on the Louisiana Pacific Railroad, truly a major achievement.

We couldn't wait every summer till Uncle Roscoe came to visit, bringing gifts and tales of seeing Lena Horne, Dorothy Dandridge, Duke Ellington, Pearl Bailey, Cab Calloway, Louis Armstrong, and Dinah Washington. It all sounded so glamorous, his tales of orange trees, the waves of the Pacific Ocean, Mexicans, vineyards — a world so distant you could be talking about Europe.

Like Uncle Roscoe, I was a reader. He gave me a copy of W.E.B. Du Bois's book *The Souls of Black Folks*. At last, facts. This book has been in print since 1903, and I had been in the land of cotton fields, bullfrogs, and ignorance. This was the history I needed, we all needed, someone black and well read, able to contradict the labels put on us of being ignorant, shiftless, apathetic little children never able to grow up.

This book put to shame their blatant racial theories. Every generation gives us heroes, and Mr. Du Bois was definitely a light for me in the dark tunnel of ignorance about our history, our heritage. The South is full of trauma and violence. Books gave me a glimpse of the past, so today makes some kind of awful sense.

The year was 1952, and the time had come for equality. More and more black men from the military were coming home from all over the world and wouldn't put up with being second-class citizens. They served in wars for this country, and yet couldn't vote or get a good job. The time had come for changes and I felt afraid.

Uncle Roscoe helped explain what had happened to us as a people after the Civil War. He talked very softly, so we listened carefully. We didn't get many chances to be around him. Uncle Roscoe said, "After the Civil War, we had no land, no house, no mule, no clothes, no job, but we were free." He told us the searing truth about how we were duped, abandoned, left to the evilness of the sharecropping existence. Uncle Roscoe said, "The beliefs that we beautiful, brown, black children were less than human shows the hatred one race can have for another." He said our fathers and brothers, our dear sweet mothers, queens from Africa, were worked to death. We were promised forty acres and a mule, but instead were freed to become homeless sharecroppers.

We were so deep in the South, behind the curtain of ignorance, cotton fields, work-scarred hands, oppression, and low wages, if any wages at all. I was always reading the want ads looking for work. What a joke! The want ads had colored and white sections. The colored ads were pitiful, mostly domestic work. I'd read the white ads, column after column of good jobs, and then back to what was available to me. Just like that, no explanations necessary. Uncle Roscoe always promised we could move to LA when we grew up — yeah, seemed like moving to the moon would be easier.

Conrad was one of my best friends at school. He stayed in trouble like me. Hell, trouble was Conrad's middle name. He cut school so many times; I knew why, of course. He had no lunch, no decent shoes, no money for books, and his uniform was just plumb worn out. Many reasons why the smartest boy I knew was delinquent.

His mama, Miss Willie Mae, was one of Mama's friends, so I feel like we had known each other forever. Yep, Conrad was another love being born; our Mamas had known each other since we were toddlers. Conrad and I grew up holding hands, laughing, playing, and just being kids. We spent afternoons in the shade of the pecan trees, talking, kissing, sweet new-love kisses, never opened our mouths, just rubs and hugs, quiet times. I loved Conrad so much. He had big dreamy black eyes and a smooth young face, mahogany brown.

He reminded me of the men of Kenya. Papa Dee had a picture of a tall brown boy who looked just like Conrad. His hair was dyed red, bright-sun fiery red, and he had a blanket draped over his shoulder. He stood alert, silent, gazing at the African landscape, his cattle in his sight, his eyes hooded by his slender hand to keep the glaring sun out, sharp, intelligent, ancient eyes.

Conrad was a bucket of trouble, born to be bad. A part of him was soft as cotton balls, dreamy as a summer sky after the rains have stopped and the world is washed clean. Conrad would tell me of his dreams, poetic for a poor boy. His family lived by the water, so Conrad had nature for his mother, snakes and birds his companions, the water his front yard. Everything I ever wanted.

We would dream out loud to each other, him fantasizing twelve-year-old-boy dreams, how he would become a pilot and fly, or be a famous ball player and buy his Mama a big house and lots of food. He said when we were grown up we would get married and be famous and rich. Fine with me, 'cause that was my plan, too. Like me, Conrad loved books; two oddballs, I swear. We would be in the shade and read aloud to each other. Kids laughed at us, but that was fine with me.

I always wrote poems and little stories in my notebooks, because I wanted to be a poet or writer when I grew up. I always had the same-old dreams, me a famous poet in New York, dark and mysterious, or in Africa finding my tribe, where I came from, a land without fear. I daydreamed of the time when we would get rich, and could buy Mama the pretty house she always wanted. Mama's favorite thing was to drive on Sundays looking at houses for sale. We usually avoided these trips. Much more fun with Daddy driving aimlessly through country roads, him searching for the good fishing spots, us playing in the woods. But oh, no, Mama's ideas were tiring. Spend hours looking at houses in fancy neighborhoods, big, arrogant two-story houses, the ones the whites have fled because the niggers are moving in. Oh, brother, give it a break! We could hardly pay the rent on time.

Conrad got caught with his brother Moses, sixteen years old and bad, stealing from the corner grocery store. Swift as lightning, he was sent away to reform school and Moses to a detention center. The beginning, the grownups said, of a life of crime and trouble. The white courts were severe on black kids. Conrad was born to lose, like being born under a strange moon.

His daddy, Mr. Albert Collins, was a drunk. He seldom worked, and it seems his main job was to beat Miss Willie Mae, a sweet little black lady, domestic worker, sort of fat, but pretty, all plump arms, dark brown eyes, mouth full and heart shaped, sweet smelling. Well, Mr. Collins beat them all. Conrad didn't really have a chance. I think it was only me he poured his heart out to. The green grass, the deep cool woods — land of snakes and wild things and me — made him happy. Yeah, I loved Conrad. He was so gentle. When the terror built up inside him it poured out like a pitcher too full. His fears poured out, and my young arms weren't big enough to hold all of him.

Grandma Emma was my lifeline, my supporter. She was an outlaw, and maybe considered rough by the better class of Negroes, but she was my heroine and my defender. My grandma could cuss so beautiful, just get her perturbed and she would let you have it. I loved it. Bad words weren't allowed in our yard. Grandma was kind and fair, but don't mess with her. Independent, and never wanting to work for anybody, she said, "Cat, I'd rather have poker games than slave silently for pennies."

I loved braiding Grandma's hair. Her daddy was an Indian, and her hair was long, thick as a rope, and soft like brushed cotton. These were my special times with her. I seemed to be the one who needed her the most, and she felt it. There was never a time she wouldn't stop whatever she was doing and listen to my stories, happy or sad, Grandma took time to listen to me and give me a big hug when I needed it.

Grandma planted many a seed of dissent in my mind. She never — I'm talking never — went to church. She dressed lavishly, and had the handsomest of men as her beaus. My favorite was Mr. Davis. Tall and well dressed, he loved my Grandma, and wanted to marry her. He asked her more than once, "Emma, marry me and stop this hustling for money. My grocery store can support us well enough." Grandma would act like she hadn't heard a word he said. Her usual reply was: "Honey I know you mean me well, but I'm too stubborn and old to be married to anyone. Hell, it wouldn't be fair to you."

I wanted Grandma to get married again so we could have a grandpa. Portia, Tilllie, and Charlotte had two grandmas and two grandpas. I just wanted one special man to be married to my grandma. But no, that was not in her plans. She never married anyone. One by one these handsome carpenters, musicians, gamblers, laborers, farmers, and painters would court her for a while and then give up. No one could capture my grandma. I once had the nerve to ask Grandma if she'd ever marry. She looked at me hard with her dark eyes and said, "Honey, love has been with me every day of my life. I loved Shorty, and that was enough for one lifetime.

"Cat," she said, "love is here now, and you are my love." She made me feel all-important and good. I still wished Grandma had someone special to hold her on winter nights, or bring her presents on her birthday. She still looked sexy, even with that pistol in her apron pocket. Grandma carried that gun in case her poker games got unruly or if any fights started. My grandma was strong, and I loved her. I felt her need. My little heart would do anything to see Grandma happy, 'cause it seems she put her youthful, rose-blossom beauty aside to make sure we survived.

Grandma was definitely not your run-of-the-mill woman, hell, no! She lived in a man's world, and didn't seem to give a damn about the consequences. Grandma was six feet tall in her bare feet. She had brown muscular arms, slender hands not afraid of work, and her eyes were so deep brown they matched her skin. Grandma's high cheekbones and long dark hair were a testament to her Choctaw father, her full mouth and attitude definitely a tribute to her African mother. She was a beautiful woman, tall, cool, and calculating. She would drink a shot of Jack Daniel's whiskey if she got upset; otherwise, Grandma didn't drink alcohol, always told me it made women too easy and aged them early.

We sure did wonder 'bout those dried green flowers Mr. Thomas brought Grandma. After rolling them into skinny cigarettes, she and her friends would send us outside to play while they smoked. Betty and I always knew something was fishy, but what? Lord knows they didn't care about us smelling their stinky old Camels or Pall Malls, whatever brand they smoked, gross to us.

This smoke caused them to giggle and sing silly songs. Their eyes would get all dreamy. We didn't know what kind of herb it was, but it smelled sweet, and it sure did have a cooling effect on those women. We girls were definitely determined to try out this magic soon as we could figure out how.

Grandma cautioned us kids never to gossip — the cops could arrest her for gambling and selling liquor. We kept secrets 'cause the brutality of the cops was well known to us. Too many men were getting their heads bloodied for far lesser crimes than this. Many women back then sold alcohol out of their front rooms, like at Grandma's. People would drop in, relax on that big soft velvet couch or sit comfortably on her big old easy chairs, and enjoy shots of whiskey, rum, scotch, mixed drinks, cold beers, soda pops, potato salad, fried chicken — you name it, you probably could get it. This was, of course, illegal, but then again, so was lynching.

Chapter 6

My Education and the Truth Didn't Agree

How could the nuns spend so much time in their black habits, their pale faces poking out of that starched white cotton head wrap that showed only their faces? The seventh grade has me bored. The nuns are so stiff. Our teacher this year is Sister Agnes, who is middle-aged and laughs a lot, different from most of our nuns. She always tells me how I can do something for the world. I am a straight-A student, but I really don't give a damn about my grades.

The nuns confuse me with their fervent love of God. They spend their lives all covered up. Their lovely necks are hidden and no tendrils of hair grace their brow, no, only sterile black and white. We girls always wondered about those nuns. We wanted to see their legs, their tits, and shoulders. Did they ever have a life? Didn't they ever have boyfriends, dance slow, and want babies? The nuns were always trying to convert us to a life of servitude. Nope, it never sounded attractive, especially the part about being married to Christ.

I hated the endless catechism classes. Where was my African religion? School opened the door to reading, and once I entered the world of knowledge, I was on my path to seeking the real truths.

Nothing was worse than the endless religion classes, reading stories of kids our age who actually saw the Virgin Mary in some poor village called Lourdes. Trust me, I could not even make up stories as far-fetched as some of the tales those nuns told us. "If you chew the holy wafer when you receive communion, the blood will flow, because the wafer is the body of Christ." I finally got the nerve to bite into the wafer, and nothing happened — another lie.

Miss Beatrice said miracles happened when the traveling healers held tent revival services. She promised to take me along to the next assembly. I really wanted to believe there was power in our prayers. Whenever I got into real trouble, like losing the rent money Mama told me to take to Mr. Albert, I was the first one to start frantically praying. It settled my mind down, and I remembered where I had left Mama's envelope.

That was sort of like a miracle. Can a blind man see again, a deaf man hear, a lame man walk, the brokenhearted laugh, the cruel become kindhearted? Seems like a miracle worker on this earth would have to work continually, because there were far too many things to fix.

School days, school days, dear old golden-rule days. April is so confusing: on the hot days we lie in the sun in our shorts and halters; moments later that old north wind bears down cold and furious, scattering the cherry blossoms all over us like soft snow. The last week of April causes us so much excitement we literally squirm in our seats at school, bored with sitting. At last, we can look ahead to summer's coming. That Friday seems to go on forever.

The weekends are our only salvation. If it gets hot, we can wear our shorts in the daytime — the nights still got cold. We can hardly wait for summer bike rides, ball games, and freedom. We counted the weeks. No more books, no more homework or catechism lessons, no more Ave Marias, goodbye school. Two months left before the languid days of summer return. We wait for golden evenings that stretch into rose-red sunsets.

Here we sit, winter uniforms still on: dreadful, unattractive, pleated, shiny, navy blue gabardine uniforms. But it will soon be time to change uniforms to the white prison school dresses we wore in the summer. Of course, the white dresses always got stained when you had your period. We would see the older girls come into the bathroom upset 'cause they stained their dresses. Holy cow, here comes another inconvenient thing to look forward to!

How we longed, lusted, to wear colorful full skirts with the stiff starched slip under that made your skirt billow out like a princess's. We yearned to grow up and wear tight skirts with slits in the back. But oh, no, only the wild public school girls were so lucky. My parents and grandmother worked extra-hard to pay the tuition, but school always felt like the army to me.

The library became my second home early. Books — shelf upon shelf of mysteries, romances, tragedies, and black history! My eyes were opened, like a rose unfurls her petals, slowly, until she is fully open and fragrant, home to bees and butterflies; so my mind was being liberated. Only through reading did I meet Indians, blacks, poor whites, tillers of the soil, blood on the ground, ancient tribes, all bashed by poverty, the manmade menace that held all these different races and tribes down. Chinese, Jews, Arabs, all over the world my young mind roamed. Books talked to me of the common thread that binds us together, life and the love of it.

In *The Grapes of Wrath*, John Steinbeck exposed to me another oppressed group, the poor white dirt farmers, so like us, so separated. The agony I suffered through that book, the enlightenment that there were noble whites, poor, displaced, unloved, looked down upon, on the move, unwelcome, displaced farmers.

Music was how we survived slavery. Singing, drumming, dancing, and storytelling helped us find beauty in the morning light, solace in the owl's call, comfort in the moonlight, dreams brought to life. Sorrows released in our songs helped carry us through the captivity; plaintive songs, melancholy, sad as a lost child, dark as a moonless night, happy as the sun filtering through the big-leafed magnolia tree, singing like a creek after the rain, music flowing from our hearts through our voices.

Every block had a singing group, and ours was no exception. Charlotte, Betty Ann, Portia, and I spent many evenings rehearsing. We were determined to be stars. Singing opened our hearts. Too bad we couldn't sing any too good. We listened to music, and it made our hearts feel happy. When the radio was on in the backyard, the little kids would dance. The blues made it easy to let the sad feelings out. Rhythm and blues made us dance fancy, and we spent hours learning new moves. Slow love songs made the nights sweet. The tender yearnings of our souls had a voice. Spirituals kept the believers fervent, as the glorious voices lifted to the heavens.

The best singers in our school were the Lewis kids. There were three of them. Betty Ann, chocolate brown, with short nappy hair and a tiny delicate body. Leroy, her older brother, was handsome as an African prince. Katie, their eldest sister, was tall, with high cheekbones, her hair a frizzy crown around her oval face. These Negroes could sing! Their mama, Miss Marion, played piano for the choir, and the whole family ruled. Yeah, they were black as night, poor as us all, but talented, able to lift us higher with their music.

Betty Ann, Charlotte, Portia, and I decided to become famous like the Chantelles. Our goal was to have money, clothes, cars — all the materialist dreams our naïve minds could invent. We figured our songs would set us free. I couldn't carry a note in a paper bag, and neither could Portia. Only Charlotte and Betty Ann could sing, so there you have us, two strong voices trying to drown out two sour notes. We had the nerve to enter singing contests held at the local black theater, but never did we win. We didn't ever get booed off the stage, but it was pretty obvious only our friends applauded for us.

We had music: spirituals, raucous blues, the boogie-woogie, rhythm and blues, and jazz. There were singing groups: the Temptations, the Pretenders, the Chantelles. Some of our singers were Josephine baker, Bessie Smith, Louis Armstrong, Pearl Bailey, Eartha Kitt, Sam Cooke, Frankie Lymon and the Teenagers, Dizzy Gillespie, Ike Turner, Junior Walker, Bessie Smith, Ma Rainey. The list goes on and on. Music excelled in us; nothing could destroy the tapestry of our soul. The strains of Mama Africa throbbed, and whether whites loved us or not, they danced to our music. Go figure.

Daddy made a deal with our landlord, and built another bedroom onto the back of the house. This expense was taken off the rent, and the room gave us more space. After Daddy built the room, with its own entrance, Mama got the brainstorm to rent that room to traveling musicians. It was Betty's and my bedroom, but we moved in with

Peggy and Linda when the musicians arrived. There were no black hotels or motels — I'm talking none — so when black entertainers pulled into Mobile, there were rooms available in private homes for the singers and crew.

When the bands played in Mobile, we always had lady singers in our home, backup singers, young, talented, with voices like birds. Sometimes they would come all the way from New York or Chicago. Mama also did the washing and ironing for the band members. We were so excited, our own singing group got the fever, and for hours we would wail, our voices as off key as they could get. The dog would sometimes howl in harmony, embarrassing.

We dreamed big. I could already see us as stars, wearing red taffeta dresses, red lips, cars, clubs, money, and fame, a way out. We dreamed big. There were always kids singing together in the evenings; on the street sides, on front porches, music was the balm for our souls, harmony our aim. Mama told us with a glare in her eye, "Don't get friendly with these ladies. They lead a fast life, and could be bad examples for you."

In spite of Mama's warnings, we did get friendly with them. They were our idols. We would gladly run to the store for their cigarettes and sodas. They would tell about Chicago where you didn't have to ride on the back of the bus and could get good jobs. I was ready to leave with them on the next bus north. Those girls would practice in their room, and I swear the very air would become sweet; the birds would hush to listen as we kids sat on the back steps in awe.

These ladies were our inspiration. There was another world other than the South! The northern musicians had to put up with a lot of humiliation to come down here to play. There were a lot of gigs they played that we blacks couldn't attend. We would listen to B. B. King sing on the radio; at the same time he would be playing at a club we coloreds weren't allowed in.

Dreams were our avenue to harmony, and peace was our goal. We were blessed with magnolia trees shading us, fireflies to delight us, and night-blooming jasmine drifting her heady perfume to delight us. Along with the beauty, we had racism and oppression as our reality, all in one bag.

Black voices blended into the summer night. Everybody's relaxing on the porch steps or the swing, or just sitting. The neighborhood guys or girls would begin singing. On and on the songs would float, the words strong, the voices out of Africa, dark and sweet like wild honey. Our mamas were all smiling, babies yawning, grandmas and the old people warmed by the purity of young souls triumphant in their innocence.

There is nothing lovelier than new buds swelling on the tree branches. Finally, we have soft days to daydream. While the teacher droned on and on, the outside air beckoned. Come on, come on, the air is sweet, and the day promises dreams fulfilled. The trees began to swell, and quickly the earth became flower-ridden, bee-filled, alive with bird songs — life was good after all.

Sunday dinners were a ritual never to be skipped. One day of the week we had the freedom to run wild through the neighborhood, shrieking with laughter. Every Sunday the dinner was at a different house. Every woman cooked her favorite recipes. Miss Lillie was known for her black-eyed peas with ham hocks, and her barbecued ribs were to die for. Miss Dot's specialty was ham glazed with pineapple and cherries. Mama's fried chicken ruled. Grandma's hot biscuits with home-churned butter and her homemade jam were a hit. Miss Lena's dishes were crab cakes and fried catfish. Miss Pat made the best butter beans and salt pork with hot cornbread. There were sweet-potato pies, chicken backs, pig's feet, red beans, and rice. We kids hated the days when they cooked chitlins. These were pigs' intestines, cleaned and cooked. They gave off the nastiest smell as they cooked.

Summer dinners were the best because of Mama's blackberry pie — hot crust baked brown with butter on top, the pastry light from the lard, and the berries cooked with white sugar and just a pinch of lemon to cut the tartness. We loved the action. There were scores of us, black, yellow, red, white-skinned Negroes — colored people they called us — all joined together. None of us had much money, but the food, the love, the singing couldn't be bought, pure soul.

The grownups were so busy partying we were able to get away with all kinds of forbidden stuff: smoking Daddy's cigarettes — wretched, but we did it — trying so hard to fit in. I'd lurch to the bathroom, all green and purple, sick as a dog, trying to be sophisticated, smoking that foul tobacco.

There was always spin the bottle when we got older. We had fun kissing boys. We pretended we hated it, when in reality we couldn't wait till the next time. The older kids played strip poker. The grownups never saw these games. They were busy drinking and partying. We couldn't wait till we were old enough.

Later in the afternoon, bellies bloated, our minds groggy from pie and home-cranked ice cream, the grownups would put on the music. In the spring and summertime we were always outside, so the music would be loud, the dancing smooth, frantic when rhythm-and-blues songs came on, slow and dreamy when the love songs would pour through the night air, fragrant, enchanting: "When I lost my baby, I almost lost my mind," or "Don't know why, there's no sun up in the sky, stormy weather." Tender, sad, loud, boisterous Fats Domino enchanting us with his song "I Found My Thrill on Blueberry Hill," or Laverne Baker belting out "Tweedlee, tweedlee, tweedlee dee, I'm as happy as can be."

Late into the night we would party, the grownups drinking moonshine, or Jack Daniel's, dancing like there was no tomorrow, the young children gazing with wonderment at the joy, young lovers dancing in the dark parts of the yard, and us nappy-headed young ones just generally kicking up our heels.

Our need for money was great. We needed cloth to cut and sew for our party dresses; we wanted patent-leather Mary Jane shoes, hair ties, and on and on. Being young entrepreneurs, my sisters, Betty and Peggy, and I opened our first refreshment stand in the heat of July, when the sidewalk stung our bare feet and the glare burned the eyes. We served lemonade, the drink of choice. In our neighborhood, most everyone walked to and from the bus stop — location, location, location.

Daddy built us a little plywood table, and if Mama wasn't too busy, we would pick blackberries, a brutal job, but sweet rewards. We each carried a gallon pail, and faithfully picked and ate berries till we were purple, our mouths stained and sticky, our fingers pricked by thorns. Money was the plan, so pick we did. We would pay Mama to bake the pies, and we'd sell slices. We ate what we didn't sell. We would play cards, comb each other's hair, play jacks, and always and forever sing.

Between doing Grandma Emma's housekeeping chores every Sunday morning, after her two days and nights of straight gambling and selling liquor and who knows what else, we were busy. The pay was good, and we could keep any money that had fallen on the floor.

I remember one Sunday morning when, after sitting in the blasted, hot-air church, we arrived at Grandma's, the screen door had the shape of a man in it. There was a big hole in the screen door — I kid you not. Seems Mr. Douglas was caught cheating. Grandma pulled out her pistol, and the man busted through the locked screen door, leaving his shape behind! Life was never dull. Between sweet lemonade and blackberry pies and illicit houses of sin, we managed to look like a million bucks in our homemade dresses, fancy shoes, and other vain goodies.

I was thirteen when Mama finally gave me permission to get my hair straightened. Brainwashed like everyone else, we all wanted to be as light to white as we could be. Foolish as it was, I couldn't wait to have straight hair; my beautiful, nappy, sandy hair was ugly to me.

The day finally arrived when I could have it done. The experience of the local beauty shop was so delicious: the loud music, the smell of hot oil and pressing irons. Hot combs were held over a gas fire till they were heated and then applied to our greased hair. The shorter your hair was the more the burns. Then they used the hot curling irons for the final touches. Oh, the things we do for beauty.

The whole atmosphere was magic to me. There were beautiful women with shiny hair and curls; the beauticians were chewing gum, laughing, singing, giggling, and gossiping. Life felt warm and soft, and I felt beautiful. The pitfall was, whenever we got our hair wet — swimming, bathing, sweating — our hair would go back to nappy. The demand for extra money to look sharp was endless now.

Corrina was one of my best ever friends — I'm talking true blue. She was short and round, with an upturned nose, a mouth made to smile, and eyes that just twinkled. Her mama was one of Mama's sewing-circle buddies; we called it the excuse-to-gossip circle, but it gave us a lot of time to hang out together.

They lived in Thomasville, down by the bay, close to the woods and the water. Corrina had three sisters: Juanita, Paulette, and Laura. Their daddy died when she was only two, so things were hard for Miss Pat. They lived in a raggedy old house; there was no porch, and the door sagged.

We loved it there. Who cares if the house is leaning and only thin shreds of gray paint remain on the battered boards? We had flowers to pick from the surrounding woods, wild azaleas, wild roses, and irises. The world was a treasure box. We picked dandelion flowers to blow at each other, wild berries to eat, bullfrogs to chase, dainty dark blue violets to smell. We tormented mean old roosters, and held baby chicks. Some days seemed so bright the world could be held in the palm of your hand, golden, magic, joy.

We captured fireflies, and searched for the crimson pitcher plant. It would only grow by the side of clear water. Mama loved this magical plant, and would pay us to bring her a root. She was a believer in the value of wild herbs. We would sit and watch the flies and bees fly down her stalk — never to get out. The birds sang by the water, the cuckoo warbled sweetly, and the little yellow finches flitted by, busily chasing nectar. Yep, we loved it there, the nights all fragrant, and the moon shining on the bay.

Miss Pat and Mama would busily dry and store herbs, then make tinctures and cough syrups throughout spring and summer. This was good for us poor souls, 'cause they'd pay us to gather wild herbs. Even through our sweatshirts and gloves the prickly nettle tops would sting. Mama said it was okay, because the oils in the plant cleaned our blood. Yeah, sure. We would do just about anything for money, 'cause movies and everything on the street cost cash we didn't have.

Corrina, Betty, and I would gather fresh dandelion leaves to be made into a tincture for the liver. Self-heal roots we would tenderly transplant, as it was wise to have healing herbs on hand. We would pluck plantain leaves for tinctures, leaving many leaves on the plant because the fresh leaves quickly pulled out infections, so easy to get in the South. We harvested beautiful vervain, cleaner of the liver, stomach, and spleen; loosestrife, the yellow willow herb, closes and cleans wounds and stops bleeding. We gathered mullein leaves, used for the lungs and throat; the yellow flowers we harvested later in the year were used to treat piles.

We went herb gathering with Miss Pat and Mama from as far back as I can remember. Baskets in hand, knives for cutting the herbs, basket for lunch, we would spend days in the woods learning the value of the herbs we tenderly gathered. Mama and Miss Pat only harvested on the right moon days. They studied herbal books and followed the old traditions. Mama's voice was muffled in the woods, but her singing was soft, and we knew she was happy doing what she loved, which made our day. Miss Pat's face was so gentle, her voice drowned by the murmur of the creek flowing by. Sitting under the branches of the cool water oaks, we sang silly songs. We were in our own church, filled with the sounds of birds celebrating the moment.

The town was pleased as punch when Mr. Sam Gaines took an interest in Miss Pat. She was a pretty lady, her face framed by a halo of fuzzy brown nappy hair. She had yellow-brown skin with the neatest freckles. Her eyes were green-brown like bird feathers. Miss Pat taught school, and did her best to keep the children together. When Mr. Sam came around, Mama and all the neighborhood hens began clucking again. What a catch, over six feet tall, brown as coffee without cream, angular face, nose finely chiseled, and lips full enough to kiss for days. Big in real estate, he drove a Lincoln Continental, and was willing to raise four girls — catch of the century.

Mama was Miss Pat's best lady, and looked so grand in her homemade lavender gown. This had to be the biggest wedding I had ever been to. The richest people in town came — the doctors, lawyers, teachers, the higher class. There was a big reception at the Mason's Hall, and it seemed to overflow with people. All the girls were dressed to kill in brand-new organdy dresses. We all wore our new patent-leather shoes and flowered hats. Mama declared, "It sure was a grand affair." Mr. Sam moved them into his brick house, and they now lived closer to school and to us.

We had more golden days to spend together. Well, as the sunny day gives way to wind and rain, the picture slowly changed. About six months into the girls' living with Mr. Sam, the changes showed up on Corrina's face. Mr. Sam was weird, a heretic — a word I had to look up in the dictionary. He didn't believe in God, any God; religion was taboo. This was a shock to Miss Pat. He never took any interest in her church, or voiced any opinions on religion until she had married him. "Mabel," Miss Pat said sadly to Mama, "I am becoming afraid of him."

Betty and I were listening in, as we did on a regular basis. Hell, we never got told anything, we just sneaked around till we heard the real news, the truth. One thing about being a child: you always can feel how things are. Grownups can smile all they want to, but kids can feel the vibrations in the air. We knew something was wrong. I almost agreed with Mr. Sam about how religion was strange, 'cause people really didn't practice the Bible. God said, "Thou shalt not kill," and war seemed to be the most popular sport around. I knew there was a brown God, angels everywhere, and rainbows forever.

Mr. Sam forbade the Bible to be in their house, and said they should not go to Catholic school or church anymore. Miss Pat was a Christian lady, and this was the beginning of conflict with her new husband. The girls were put in public school, where, of course, I would have jumped for joy to go. But maybe the fun goes when you are forced to do something. Miss Pat seemed to lose her backbone. She quit her church; fine with that, but the girls and Miss Pat were not allowed to hobnob with many people. Luckily, they were still allowed to play with us.

Once Corrina came to spend the night. Later, after everyone was asleep, she told me quietly, "Cat, Mr. Sam found the Bible my Daddy gave me, and that mean old man made me sit at the kitchen table and burn that book, page by page. The fire burned a hole in that new table. Then he beat me with a belt buckle." My heart jumped into my mouth. Here I thought Mama was the bride of Frankenstein, forcing Bible lessons, threatening us with beatings, God and punishment, hell and fire. Holy moly! Along comes another weirdo, who beats you if you *do* read the Bible. Go figure.

That was the beginning of the girls being beat all the time. Things came to a head when Corrina came to school all scarred on her face with the lashes from the belt buckle, and her older sister, Juanita, had a black eye from being struck with a whip. The principal called the police in, and Mr. Sam — the big, black, important, Lincoln-driving man — threw Miss Pat and the girls out.

Mama and her sewing-circle buddies all went over to help Miss Pat move. They stayed with us for a while. It was fun. We had a house full of girls, and we must have giggled halfway through the nights. But it was a big lesson in the strangeness of the grown-up mind.

As a child, people's feelings were like a cloak of colors to me. All my friends — hell, lots of strangers — had lights over them, especially if they were nice to us. Portia, Tillie, Dorothea, Charlotte, and Corrina all had streams of color that flowed from the tops of their heads and down over their shoulders. Red, orange, purple, lavenders, silver. I swear it on the Bible. If Portia was feeling low, her frizzy hair would be all limp, her mouth turned down, and her cloak got all silver and gray. When the sun was shining and her world was good, she always had orange and red over her. I told the girls this, and they laughed at me and said I was a hopeless dreamer. Maybe so, but they had the most delightful showers of color over their shoulders.

Mama's friend, Miss Dot, was a trouble to me. Her colors were most always gray and purple. She might have on a red dress, red lips, shiny, black glossy hair, and high heels, but her eyes so many times were the color of the water on a stormy day.

She and my mama would whisper in the living room, telling us to go out and play, but no way, José, I loved to listen. Mama in her house-dress and pretty apron was the never-ending listener; she always had time to listen, and so did I. Miss Dot told Mama, "My Lord, Mabel, I swear I am tired of getting hit by him. I can't afford to leave him, I got nowhere to go." Seems Miss Dot's husband, Mr. Johnny, was always beating on her. In those days, this seemed so common, almost normal. The women would tsk and tsk, but poor black women's rights were not respected.

Nobody should hit Miss Dot; she was like a newly opened flower, a wild azalea just beginning to change from gray-pink to scarlet. Her body was long and lean, and her arms were muscular. Her lovely face looked like some great artist had sculpted it. She was the only child of a good couple up in Jackson, Mississippi. Mr. Johnny promised on the Bible to be good to her, and I guess he loved her, but his hands became weapons. Miss Dot was like a bird that had left the nest too quickly — she never, ever had a chance to fly. She had three young children, and did domestic work.

When we went to Miss Dot's house for Sunday dinner, she would say, "Hey, good-lookin', what you got cookin'," or "What's up, buttercup?" I would look into her eyes and feel like I was in the coolest, greenest woods, by a clean-running creek. When she hugged me, the love floated through her skin and came into mine. I could feel the warm love feeling me up with joy. That's how she was.

Miss Dot looked like a queen, even in a housedress, but beat her Mr. Johnny did. He worked hard as a laborer, and in all fairness was a good man. He had a tall, ample body, broad neck, red-brown skin, and boy, was he handsome! His big hands and wrists showed the work he did. He seemed kind, but the wicked scratches, slaps, and bruises on Miss Dot were black and blue. She had nowhere to turn; her family was in Mississippi, and the cops could care less about some nigger beating his woman — saved them the trouble.

Such a mess! That's what I get for listening to unexplained, un-fixable, grown-up trouble. Mr. Johnny — Red he was called — was active in his church and respected. They owned their own home, and seemed the pillars of society. What a joke! The more I listened, the more the cynic in me was being born.

The night hangs heavy on the hills, dampness covers the earth, and spring seems a vague promise. I have never loved February, the month before spring really grandly announces herself, spreading color wherever she walks. Only the daffodils and wild violets peeking through the sodden earth gave us hope.

We spent the winter evenings huddled around a little gas heater, way too small to heat our house, and we were never warm enough. The days were short, and the nights full of dreams, of darkness, and sometimes fears. How can fear become so familiar to a little child?

From the moment I was born, some kind of war's been going on, and as far as I can understand, man has always hated man. I'd hold so tight to Mama's knee, her eyes as deep as the black night before the first stars appear, and her face as sad as a Louisiana funeral. She'd look almost bewildered, her dark eyes holding my attention. "Honey," she'd say, "this life can do you harm. Oh, baby, life can do you harm."

How we hated war. Born in 1941, I was too young to know when the atomic blasts went off, but when I got older, I feared attacks from other nations and learned to hate the Germans and Japanese. War movies were gross to my sisters and me; rather, we endured grossly pathetic comedies where we were depicted as maidservants or dumb footmen. No wonder Lena Horne, Sarah Vaughn, Dorothy Dandridge, and other lovelies gave us some kind of self-esteem. With their faces made up and their hair pressed, they were our queens. These women were singing and acting their hearts out, giving us a belief that indeed we too were beautiful.

The sun spread crimson and lavender streaks across the fading sky. As evening crept in, the clouds slowly relinquished their colors, and dark purple faded into gray — the beginning of the long, cold February night. Peace should prevail; waves of warmth should fill our souls, but no, just war and the rumors of war. Now the news tells us that Russia is the new nuclear enemy. For Christ's sake! We had to practice how to duck under our desks and crouch in case the nuclear bombs fell.

Give me a break! Daddy had already told us about the tens of thousands of people — I'm talking innocent children, women, old people — incinerated in Japan, and the millions of Jews and minorities gassed to death in Germany, and they're telling us to crawl under a desk? Oh, brother! Fear is that unseen thing that lives in the chest and spreads slowly through every vein. Some kids seemed unaffected, playing cards, reading comics, going to movies, and singing. I, the perplexed fool who read too many books, was scared.

When did war begin? Was it when we were still cave people, just evolved from the apes? Was it when the neighboring tribes were marauding and killing? Was it when the Romans spread Christianity? Was it the Spanish Inquisitions? When will war end? These were heavy thoughts for a young girl.

Mardi Gras always came at the end of February, and for a week, all heaven broke loose. There were floats with masked people in grand costumes, throwing us candy. The regal torchbearers lit the streets at night, and the black marching bands whipped ass. We were made to march at the back of the parade. With their syncopated beats, our drum majorettes and drum majors were the best.

Mardi Gras meant open houses with big steaming pots of gumbo, fish, and chicken dishes. People put aside all worries for that short time. We had our own black parades on Davis Avenue, the best marching bands, and all the colored civic clubs trying to outdo each other and delight us kids. The big-wheel black people had fancy balls and exclusive dinners; we little people just partied like there was no tomorrow.

Chapter 7

Childhood's End

Time marches on. I am thirteen now, and am beginning to see life more clearly. This old world just keeps on turning, and the world still seems a trouble to me. Maybe it's Mama's sighs for the things we don't have. Maybe it's the end of winter, and my young skinny-girl self just wants to feel warm again.

Lonely, lovely, new-moon night, hanging like a golden sliver in the evening sky. Venus under her, promising love and goodness, prayers answered. March is cold in the daytime, and the night makes you feel sorry for the poor and homeless. The first time I can remember seeing the hoboes, I was intrigued. Betty asked me, with fear in her eyes, "Cat, who are those men with old raggedy clothes coming in the yard?"

Mama came onto the porch and greeted them warmly. They were both of them older men. One looked discouraged, but the younger of the two had a spark of promise in his eyes, and greeted Mama. "Good day, miss. We're looking for work of any kind. We're traveling around and just need a hot meal or money enough to buy a dinner." There were lots of hoboes in that time. They rode the freight trains, and would look for work.

Mama was kind, and always found something for them to do for a hot meal and fifty cents. She always wished she could do more. They had no warm bed, not even clean blankets. We felt sorry for them. When the night came creeping in, the cold settled, and the wind whistled and howled through the trees. Mama said, "See, Cat, there is always someone needing food or shelter. We have to be grateful for our warm beds and for having enough food to eat."

I can feel it in my bones, the days are getting longer, and the light is returning. Every day another bird song, another flower peeking up through the earth, and our winter-tired, cold selves begin to smile. I never knew too much about Mama's daddy or mama. Her name was Sherry, and she died when Mama and her brother and sister were young children. Mama's Daddy was named Albert, and Mama hardly ever talked about him, no matter how I'd beg her. Most of my friends had grandparents, and I admit to being jealous. Grandma was our only link to our past, and we loved her.

We only had one faded picture of Mama when she was twelve, leaning against an old Ford. She was so young and unscarred, a bright smile lighting her face; the world seemed to be hers for the asking. When Mama met Daddy, he was her prince, her hero. I don't know how much love she got as a child, but Daddy was her promise of love, children, and security.

We never had a camera, so pictures of our family were few and far between. They were treasured, framed and hung with pride in our living room, when we were lucky enough to have one; otherwise, they were hung up in Mama's room. Whenever Mama was out to shop or work, Betty and I would open her world, her polished cedar chest. Mama's cedar chest smelled of mothballs and lavender. It was big enough to lie down in if it was empty. We would sift through her dreams: stained photographs, yellowed papers, visible memories. We would look at the little faded picture of our first brother, dead as an infant; our birth certificates were crumpled and faded.

Mama saved locks of our hair tied with ribbons, each in a separate little satin bag. That chest held Mama's wedding certificate, her wedding dress, our baby shoes, Daddy's first bankbook, a handmade baby quilt made by Aunt Hattie for Mama's firstborn, faded pictures of Grandma Emma and Shorty, one of Daddy as a young boy, and one picture of Mama's family. All the images were brown and creased with age. Everything Mama valued was kept there.

Everything in that chest smelled of mothballs, lavender, and old, fragrant dried roses. Anything important went into the chest: a dance program, a canceled train stub, she had it—a memory box, holding dreams and disappointments. It was like traveling through time. Her memories were held in material swatches of lace or dog-eared papers, tears and fears and lovely dreams, caught in the polished chest. Does anyone keep a cedar chest anymore?

The chest brought back distant sounds from another time. Betty and I would dream of years ago when we were freshly made and reality was brand new. Our first memories are Mama's breasts. We were the lucky ones and were fed breast milk. The losers had sugared baby formula, that modern scheme to dry women's breasts and sell a substitute for nature's finest food. I kid you not, women stopped breast-feeding, and the bottle became the fad. Naturally, most of us coloreds kept on nursing—to hell with the store, the milk flowed freely. Many black women had jobs as wet nurses, meaning they would breast-feed the white child along with their own, lucky little kid to be nursed by a black woman.

As March boldly strides into the southland, life explodes. Birds that were so distant through the gray sullen winter all at once are busy singing and building nests. The hummingbirds are frenziedly seeking nectar. All through the woods and hills, the magic of spring is spreading her new green and lavender beauty all across the ground, like a grand queen spreading her cloak. We were indeed enchanted.

The glamorous tree-sitting days of March have begun, and my girlfriends and I spend hours with our hair flying, sweaters fluttering, smiles bright, hanging on to that old oak tree, as the March winds rock our boat. Those days were spent either in quiet dreaming or vibrant talk of the future. We would predict how many children we'd have, their names, and all our futures, mapped out in that tree. We would dream of handsome husbands who would go happily off to work whistling, leaving us quite serene to be good wives and mothers.

How simple it was to indoctrinate us. We planned out rosy futures. Portia said, "Just think, we will be neighbors and best friends, have houses with roses everywhere, raise our babies together, and cook good hot meals." It sounded good, but each of us in our heart of hearts, red upon red, and vision upon vision, must have felt as I did.

There had to be more. Hell, we were poorer than church mice; only a couple in our gang had a chance to go off to college, start a new life, learn the higher concepts of the world so they would be able to teach or in some way make a difference. Nope, not me. I could see no way to go to college. I figured, even with a partial scholarship there was just no way I could afford clothes and books. I didn't talk about this with Grandma. She was already paying tuition for us. Hell, that old tree in March was our council tree.

One thing about a small town, the news spreads fast. Miss Terrecina came over and quickly began talking to Mama. "Oh, Lord have mercy, Mabel, Belinda is dead." Mama looked like she might faint as she held on to the door frame and told Miss Terrecina to come on in. Betty and I were just listening, the breath taken from us. Belinda had killed herself, hanged herself in a closet — and she'd been pregnant, too. I nearly passed out.

The news rippled like lightning, like a wildfire, through our town on the loveliest of early April days. Bees dizzy from nectar are iridescent streaks in the bright sunny air, and the wildflowers carpet the land. Why, oh why, on this beauty-filled, blue sky, golden sun-kissed day would Belinda hang herself? Wasn't there anybody close to call out to?

My thirteen-year-old mind was full of questions. Where was Belinda's angel — did she try to stop her? That sweet angel was supposed to protect Belinda, not lead her home early. She was only sixteen and had just begun life; she was supposed to live till she was full of wonder and grandbabies. Maybe her angel went with her, saw that her young girl's heart was too destroyed, her body too young to be a mama. On this windy April funeral day, this is the only way I can breathe.

Seems Belinda found herself pregnant, and horror upon horrors, now that funny, short, full-hipped, laughing-eyed little darling is gone. She was always helping us younger girls. She gave us tips on fingernail polish, hairstyling, and fashion. She didn't seem to mind hanging with us. Her sister, Belle, was my age and a close buddy. We adored her pretty older sister, full of giggles and always singing.

Belinda was pregnant from her daddy, taken by her daddy. The news was supposed to be secret, but we girls heard all the gossip. We wept a river of tears, especially Belle. Boy, did we girls want to beat up Mr. Paul, a dark brown man, tall and skinny, his nervous eyes always shaded, sunny or not. He never gave us kids the time of day. His pretty wife, Miss Billie Lee, was a good soul. The day was hot, and the bees were droning, but the only sound I heard was the clock ticking and my heart beating way too fast.

But that turquoise day in April, while the bees droned, Belinda hanged herself, and the day cried. The dogs barked, and a red-tailed hawk just kept circling and circling and circling over that house. Like a bird lost in flight, a sailor on a stormy night, a mother seeking her lost child, she was feeling lonely, oh, so lonely.

Another funeral, and I am getting sick of grown-up ways. Mr. Paul should be in jail, yet nothing is being said. Charlotte is so angry her eyes flash. "Cat, we girls don't get treated right at all. Nobody is doing a thing." Portia is so sad; her eyes are all puffy and red from crying, and she asks us, "How come they don't talk about this in school? Don't we have rights?" Nope, nothing was said outside of secret gossip. The priest gave a lame talk, and that was it. Our friend was laid to rest, and the days were dreary for months.

Then May arrived in all her splendor. Northern Alabama has been visited by another tornado, and rain and the leftover winds from the Birmingham area pelt us. The lilac trees are beginning to bud, the camellias are in full bloom, their lovely red, pink, creamy white flowers sparkling from their dark shiny leaves. The wisteria are budding, and soon the world will be riotous with color. We wait for summer's freedom.

School would soon be over for the summer, and we were eager for freedom and catfish dinners. Honeysuckle blossoms beckoned to us to pull stamen from flower and suck the sweet nectar. Flying kites and eating peanut butter and homemade jelly sandwiches in the shade of the fig tree would keep us happy. Lying around on fig-tree branches so low and wide, we dangled limply like monkeys.

We idled away hours, the sun filtering through those big, green leaves, all the rough spots of life calmed down and vanished. The sweetness in the air was a balm to our souls. Our dreams were bigger than life. In our poor world, we lived large in our dreams. The clouds put on a show for us, changing from birds to beasts as they sailed across the blue spring day.

Davis Avenue was one of the main thoroughfares for us coloreds. Our school was on one end, and the public school on the other. I would have gladly traded my soul to the devil to go to Carver High. No, our school was Heart of Mary. Give me a break! No wonder the public school kids loved to kick our pious asses. Of course their football team beat us unmercifully, but their drum majorettes and marching bank whipped us, too. We had to wear these suits down to our knees, while their sexy little shorts were so gorgeous. Oh, the agony of the Catholic life!

There was nothing left to do. May had arrived, the days were golden and warm, and school had become unbearable. The nuns in their thick black cotton habits had beads of sweat over their lips and foreheads, and they grew far too grouchy. We used to say they were horny, but nevertheless, the days were too long to be schoolroom-bound. The seventh grade was the beginning of just plain skipping school, past the time when we would pretend to be sick, and then have to stay in bed all day. Past the hooky-playing days, nope, this was it.

Charlotte was my friend, tall, tan, and mischievous. I was too scared to skip school again. Mama had found all the forged notes from school when I had lied and didn't go. I was in serious trouble. Mama warned me, "Cat, you lie one more time, and you'll be at home forever." I wanted to obey Mama, but temptation won. We would skip school, meet at Charlotte's house after her parents went dutifully off to work, and lie around till three. After we learned the game, we got bold enough to go to movie matinees, or just saunter downtown all day. Mostly we just lounged around. I think we secretly enjoyed the intrigue, the fun, and the lies. Nobody cared, even when we were caught and got suspended from school and grounded. We didn't give a rat's ass — school was hot and boring, hooky was fun. We had no remorse, just anger at getting caught.

We had all been friends since we were toddlers: Charlotte, Portia, Corrina, Tillie, and Betty Ann. Sister Vincentia, her skinny nose red from the Alabama sun, her mouth a barely open pink gash, and her lips skinny as a pencil line, used to say, "Birds of a feather flock together," meaning we were all bad and encouraged each other. Yep, damn right, we did! We suffered the agony of wearing uniforms all alike, and we were punished if we ever dared wear a dress to school. Wearing a dress, hell, that was a cinch, just a reprimand.

We got so bad we enjoyed the thrill of stealing at the dime store, and hated the scandal of the stolen costume jewelry being found under Portia's bed. We played endless poker games, became pros at swearing, stole our parents' cigarettes, and made endless stupid phone calls to boys. This was the beginning of shamelessly flirting, and wishing for the day when we would need bras. Yep, life was good, but we weren't.

My father was a quiet man, quick to hit, and a victim to his own desires, but many times after he'd had his dinner, he would talk to us over his coffee. He would still have his painter's suit on because he had a second job to go to, so these moments were to be savored.

I don't know what brought it on, but Daddy told us about that hanging of Mr. Willie. It was a lazy afternoon, the birds were singing in the treetops, and the flowers were in full bloom. Daddy was feeling talkative, sitting in his easy chair, and it felt like it was a good time to listen, oh, yeah, felt like a good time to be there.

Daddy looked thoughtful as he stirred his coffee. He was reading an article in *Ebony* magazine about the National Association for the Advancement of Colored People. The civil rights movement was the biggest topic of conversation. Daddy said, "Seems like it took years for us to get to this point." He asked us, "Did I ever tell you kids about Mr. Willie Brown?"

Daddy didn't talk too much, so when he decided to tell us about our history, we listened. He told us: "Willie Brown was a good friend of almost everybody in Clarksdale. He had a big smile, and a strong lean body to work a good honest day." Mr. Brown was Grandma's neighbor in Clarksdale, and his wife was her good friend. Daddy looked sad when he said, "Willie had every reason to be alive. He owned a piece of land, and had a good wife. She was pretty enough to make anyone smile. Pauline was her name, and if Cleopatra had a sister it was she!

"Seems like not everybody was as pleased as us when Willie bought his land. Some folks felt he was out of his place and getting uppity." Daddy's eyes looked cold as he told us this tale. Maybe it was reminding him of his own father. We were all glued to our seats, hanging on to his every word.

"The Klan boys visited his home one late June night. The moon was full, and the energy of the heavens was howling. Willie and Pauline were home alone, so there was nobody there to help them. They dragged him from his house, threw him into a pickup truck, and took him right outside of town where they hung his body night and day. They made sure everybody saw him — what a shame on the living. Poor, poor Willie, happened one more time, fallen angels all around us, they took a good soul and hung him." All of us were silent after Daddy told his tale. Even the birds stopped singing. But it felt like it was a good time to listen.

I was thirteen when Daddy told us that tale. It made me moody and sad. The world I was living in was not at all like the movies or the radio shows of the day, where life was grand, every girl had patent-leather slippers, went to church on Sunday, got married when she was older, and lived happily ever after. Daddy was growing us up too fast; life in the make-believe stage was so comforting, and here was my daddy telling us scary tales about lynchings. We were still riding in the back of the buses. My childhood crumpled.

My daddy made sure to tell us as much about politics as he could. He always said, "Study hard, read everything, only knowledge can free you children." Back then I could only wonder, as freedom seemed so far away, another state maybe, but living in the Deep South? I felt trapped.

As a child feels the night's loneliness, I suffered the pangs of discontent, social, moral, and spiritual. As the moth circles the light, getting closer and closer, daring to jump in no matter the danger of the heat, I searched out the truth. George Washington, the first president, had slaves and grew hemp, for Christ sake, and most Indians were victims of genocide. Where were the answers, when school kept us in line, and discouraged us from questioning our history books?

I hated school; too many uniforms, too many gray-assed rosary days, eyes bent, kneeling on some hard pew like a sinner. Catholic school introduced me to dark demons that lived in a place called hell, a place of hot coals and everlasting fire. Oh, my Brown God, too much hell, purgatory, and limbo. School uniforms on Africans made captives of our bodies but not our minds.

Finally, justice! School is closing in two weeks and the delicious summer will be here. Somehow I pulled it off and didn't get totally expelled. I got suspended three times this year, and got two written notes to take home to my parents, but I made it. Plus, I, the rebel, made straight A's in class and D's in deportment. I'm glad schoolwork is easy for me. It's just trying to seek out the truth that gets me in trouble.

I have just finished reading *To Kill A Mockingbird* by Harper Lee, and am once again reassured that to question is truly to be intelligent. I swear most of my classmates seem to live for recess time, and don't really worry like me. I confess I love flirting and hanging out, too, but in my deepest heart, I feel way too old for my age.

I worked for weeks sewing my eighth-grade graduation dress. I bought a Simplicity pattern, and felt proud to be able to sew my own dress. It was so lovely: white polished cotton, formfitting, with a dashing slit in the back. It was quite elegant, I thought, with short sleeves and the neatest little waistband. I proudly tried it on to show to Mama as soon as I had finished hemming my masterpiece. She didn't say a word, just got up from her chair and tore my dress off my back, tore it to shreds and started screaming at me, "What do you want to look like, a whore?" She said it was too tight, too sexy looking; then she proceeded to slap my face, lonely, lonely me.

Of course I wanted to look sexy. Hell, we were inundated with pictures of lovely women. *Jet* magazine always had a centerfold of some beautiful girl in a bathing suit. To be desired, to have tits, boys calling after us — what else matters at thirteen? I look too sexy? Come on, Mama, you look sexy with your pressed waved hair and shoulder-pad suit, all tight and formfitting. And your nylon stockings with the black lines running straight up the back of the legs look sexy, too. Your beautiful hats with netting over the eyes, red lips, rouge, powder, and perfumes are sexy.

Yeah, she beat my ass as Daddy and my brothers looked on. Betty and Linda, their eyes were sad and fearful. Peggy stood there crying her little brown eyes out. The next day Grandma brought me a white dress with a full skirt and a Peter Pan collar. I detested it.

I read that in the days of slavery the master would tie a slave down to the ground, stake his hands and feet, tie him on his stomach, and literally beat him to death. Or if he just got a whipping, he was beaten and then salt was rubbed into his cuts. The women were routinely raped, and humiliation was our meal. It took me years to forgive Mama, to search my roots, go back to the brutality Mama was trying to protect me from. Whatever she had seen in her childhood, what was it she wanted to shield me from?

Mama never gave answers. We just cried when she whipped us for whatever reason. Bless my sisters, my angels who wept with me; I wept with them. We would laugh till we hurt our sides, run till we were breathless, gamble, lie, flirt, cuss, and, most important, back each other up. We told one another our fears and sorrows while braiding each other's hair. There was always tomorrow, and I knew I would run away.

My daddy was a handsome man, with light freckles on his cheeks and nose. His hair was brown and wavy with a widow's peak. His brown-flecked green eyes looked like marbles to me, cat's eyes. We lived so secluded in our little world. I remember my daddy's work shoes, his thick wrists, and how callused and swollen his hands were from the cement jobs he would do after a whole day of painting houses. The smell of paint and turpentine drifted from his clothes at the end of a hot workday. His painter's white shirt and pants and his work shoes were always color stained. Daddy's gruff pride in us made us want to succeed. Even though he gambled, caroused, cheated, lied, and whored around, he never left Mama, because surely we would have perished.

Combined with Mama's sewing jobs, Daddy's fishing, hunting, painting jobs, gambling, and God knows what else kept us from starving and a roof over our heads. There were days when the cupboards were bare, but Mama never gave in to despair. She would give a little sigh, lean her head slightly to one side, and her eyes were bottomless pools. On those days we were unusually well behaved and careful not to ask for more food.

My soul felt troubled one summer evening as Grandma and I were swinging on the front porch. I felt the need to ask her, "Grandma, is there really a place called hell? Am I going to burn in fire forever? And what about you, Grandma? You don't even go to church." Grandma gave me one of her long sighs and slowly told me, "Honey, hell and heaven are right here on earth. Paradise and hell live side by side. Life is a lesson to learn, and that lesson is love, everlasting love. There is no hell, darling. Only the wicked fear death. Remember, Cat, we come from paradise and that's where we return. There is no death. Our souls live forever with the fairies and angels. Otherwise, how could you children hold eternity in your eyes?" My Grandma was indeed my lifeline.

I always felt in my heart that I must be all right because I saw my brown-skinned guardian angel at the head of my bed. I had gone to sleep so troubled. The world I knew, soft and clean, with silver stars — even these things of beauty couldn't put out the fire. I was old enough to feel the pain of poverty, be hurt by mean and uncaring people, and endure the indignities we all had to suffer.

I remember my sisters all being asleep while I hung on the window-sill and sang softly to the spirits who I knew were always out there to send me a friend. Just before dawn, that magic time between sleep and waking, I sat up quickly. A young brown woman was standing next to me on the left side of my bed. She was wearing a lavender-and-blue gown, and heaven was in her eyes.

She put her fingers to her lips to motion to me not to speak. As I watched her, she backed away and then vanished. I saw paradise. No one believed me, but that was okay. Her visit gave me the strength to endure.

How come life couldn't always be as still as a summer afternoon, as cool as iced tea served in tall flowered glasses with real glass stirrers? Little things gladden the heart. I learned early, catch the moments of rapture as they filter through your fingers, and bathe in the golden times.

Aunt Sunny died of a heart attack when I was thirteen years old. They were gambling in our living room, just Daddy, Aunt Sunny, our next-door neighbor Mr. Williams, Miss Elise from down the street, and Mr. Harry, just a friendly game. Mama and Uncle Rogers were sitting on the front porch, talking quietly, fanning themselves in the humid air. We kids were bored, too early to go to bed, too late to be outside playing — loitering, Mama called it. Just one of those jasmine-filled, whippoorwill-song nights, no breeze except for the fan.

We were in our bedroom playing dominoes when Miss Elise started screaming. We heard the rush of feet, Mama was moaning, and Aunt Sunny was carried out to Mr. Harry's car and driven to the colored hospital. All through the black night we sat up. Grandma, soft and quiet. Her sister, her best friend, lay dying. Soon enough, just before the night departed, as the last tinge of black was fading into purple dawn, Aunt Sunny passed away.

Praise be! She'd been drinking and gambling, doing the things she loved the most. She and Uncle Rogers never had any kids. I remember how sad his smile looked after she left. That giantess of an aunt, that former plantation worker, died in her dancing shoes, and this old world just kept on walking and talking. As for me, my heroine was gone. The song left the birds for days, the shadows in the night held her shape, and the old night wind blew her name all through the lane.

Did you ever dream you could fly? No wings, just the currents to drift on, over mountains, valleys, rivers, oceans, busy cities, avenues, and cars. Life goes on as usual, only you are over it all, effortless, gliding joy.

Many times, flying dreams gave relief, when the burdens of life accumulated, like dark sins, stains on my soul from my forefathers, the ancestors I will never be allowed to know. The horror of reading about those damn slave ships, where Africans were stripped down and shipped like cattle. The dead were just thrown overboard, not like humans. Here I am, thirteen years old, and have already read about Bayard Rustin, Mahatma Gandhi, Martin Luther King, Jr., and I am here, young, without a past, looking desperately for a future.

Both my grandmas were pretty much abused, taken too early, left too soon, no past, what future? We were never really given high aspirations; we were definitely not going to college. Even with full scholarships, there was no money for clothes, food, and the bare necessities. Not too much hope. How I secretly envied my friends who already knew they were going to do well, go to college, be teachers, nurses, doctors.

It was all about money or the lack of it, a bitter pill to swallow.

Downtown Mobile was tense and tight. There were early talks and meetings about demonstrations against Woolworth's dime stores, where we were not allowed to eat, plus no bathrooms. Hell, the time had come! The wind roared loud, and the evening sunset sometimes looked too red and angry. There was complete silence in my house. Mama refused to let us get involved; couldn't blame her, but young blood boils hot, and damn it, the time had come to speak up.

Think what a shock it was when we got old enough to realize most of the white-sand beaches were definitely not for us. Yeah, the signs clearly stated white or colored on the beaches. No problem, just another stinking slap in our faces. I was so weary of injustice. I was young and beautiful and should have been able to swim in your private water and lie down upon your white man's beach. Please, even the beaches were segregated! Wonder why I wished that I could fly, why I cried; why tomorrow didn't always seem bright. Dreams could be too full of dark fears. How I longed to fly away.

I was so glad the woods were behind us, deep and green. We'd walk, always looking for wildflowers, purple and pink wild ginger, nettles, sorrel, wild orchids so little you had to get on your knees to look at the regal ladies all attired in beige and royal shades of purple and burgundy. Beauty on the ground, birds everywhere.

We would look for the right tree to climb on, our favorite occupation, tree climbing. The June afternoons were heavy with sunshine the color of daffodils filtering down upon us. We'd all take our favorite branch and get comfortable, baloney sandwiches and Cokes in hand. We'd feel the earth rise and fall, hear the distant dog bark in the heat of the afternoon.

The bees droned slowly on and on, the goldenrod waved yellow and gold wands in the wind, and the birds sang, avoiding the tree we were on. Heaven, the sky was so blue it looked unreal, like the sea turned upside down, and time seemed suspended, like a beautiful purple iris. There is no measure of time when the heart is filled with the beauty of the moment.

Blessed is the child who has a favorite tree to climb on, and from that lofty perch, so close to the clouds and the warm summer breezes, a place to dream. Some have tree houses. My girlfriends and I scaled the old oak tree at the end of our block and surveyed our world. Who doesn't love a tree? Surely the city child must have the occasional tree pushing up through the cement, or in the parks.

Did you ever hug a tree? We always did. If you hug long enough, I swear the soul of the tree will talk to you, and you can feel her heartbeat. It doesn't matter if you can't encircle her trunk, just plant your feet gently on Mother Earth, and hold your body close enough to feel her bark, sometimes smooth, other times rough. Smell the pitch oozing, let that tree talk to you, let the flow of life run through you. She has endured storms and floods, and seen many a person pass on and others appear. This tree has gathered songs in her hair, and been the refuge of the birds and wild things. That oak tree was our home away from home. Everything in the lane looked distant, and we girls had the world to ourselves.

I grew to detest the pleated navy blue jumper, white blouse, and ugly black brogan shoes. We weren't given the freedom to wear the bright colors we reveled in. The public school girls could wear tight skirts, low-cut blouses, and makeup, foxy girls. We captives of the catholic school were held down. Who ever invented the uniform, some prison warden?

Our church was painted white, and had a steeple with a bell on it. It was nothing too grand. The school was right next to the church, and the kindergarten, grade school, and high school had separate wood buildings, just functional. We were having our last assembly before eighth grade graduation. Father Albert made his grand entrance. He was a nervous little man, and he and I didn't like each other. Oh, boy, by now I had garnered quite a reputation for rudeness and being a troublemaker.

In the eighth grade I was humiliated in front of our school assembly. I raised my hand when Father Albert asked if we had any comments regarding going to a special Mass at the cathedral for graduation. I asked, "Why do we have to go to Mass at the whites' grand church, and kneel and kiss the bishop's ring, while he stands there like a king in satins and brocades, wearing his fancy shiny shoes? Kneel to kiss his ring? Why? What is God like?"

At this point, Father Albert asked me to please sit down, and to come to see him after assembly if I had any more questions. He said, "Cat, this is not the time to discuss this, please take a seat." In that great cathedral, we were herded into the back pews, and most of us had to stand. There wasn't enough room for us all.

I went to Father Albert's study after the assembly and was told, "Please don't make any more trouble, Cat, or there will be serious consequences." Father Albert said, "I have no other option then to tell you that if you keep up this type of harassment, you will not be welcome back. You will not be allowed to graduate with your class, even though you passed your grades. The graduation at the cathedral will be minus one person — you." I had dared to speak openly in assembly, and was suspended for the first, but of course, not the last time.

Portia, Claudette, Tillie, Kali, all my friends loved it. Hell, all the kids knew I was right. Why did I open my big mouth and say it? Mama and Daddy were getting worried about me. They claimed I was asking for trouble. The persecution of blacks was accelerating quickly. There were more crosses being burned, more murders and beatings. More and more blacks were doing more and more time in jail for minor crimes related to illiteracy and poverty.

I hated poverty, that frequent visitor at our door. Sentiments like this got me thrown out of class so much I swear I was a yo-yo. Not to mention the corporal punishment when I got home. But even then, bruised and soul-weary as I was, my heart kept beating, strong and true.

We were starting to protest vocally; no more sullen stares, we were getting ready to stand up. Like a baby beginning to stand, to walk, eventually to run free and wild, we were standing up. The after-blow of slavery was rebellion, and my generation felt, smelled, the winds of change. Mama wanted me to be silent. After all, I was an honor-roll student, and to talk back meant possible trouble at home, but I was only thirteen, and it was a small price for getting something off my chest.

Yep, growing up ain't all it's made out to be. The older I get, the less simple things make sense to me. Human actions astound me. Nature and I understand each other just fine. I can live with the seasons, dark winters that try the soul, and long nights of solitude. I embrace glorious summer days, when heaven opens her arms and embraces us with her soft breezes, her melody of bird song, running streams, and fresh fish caught from a clean river.

Mama said I lived too much in make-believe land. "Girl, put down that book and go outside. It's a beautiful day, and you are in this house lounging. Cat, stop reading so many books. Work more, and think less." This was easy for her to say. The newspapers were screaming out bigotry. Our governor, George Wallace, wouldn't obey the courts and let us into the schools of our choice. Hell, just to vote, just to eat where we wanted, was — is — a struggle.

It was like living in a shadow world sometimes, so many questions, so few answers. Sex was strictly taboo, not to be discussed, no explanations, so to the dictionary we went. We looked up words like *menstruation, period, orgasm,* and *pregnancy*. We were never allowed to question, only told that in our early teens we would get our period and could get pregnant, so don't fool around with boys. Ha! Mess around we did — love notes and endless silly phone calls. We were indeed simple, with our slow dances and flirting.

We fell in and out of love with all the handsome boys. We started going to parties at friend's houses. The music, sweet and low, gave us a chance to slow dance. These parties were the perfect place to make out in the backyards. I finally got a chance to French kiss!

Tyrone Bates was handsome and smooth. All the girls wanted him, and I was on cloud nine. The music was hot, and we were all groping, panting, the boys making our panties wet. Sex was forbidden, and not to be discussed. What a shame. There were so many early pregnancies, a disgrace to the girl, and if the boy didn't claim the baby, there were early hardships. No one was to blame; our culture was so broken down by Christianity and displacement, what else could evolve?

How could we, buck naked, big-butted, dark-eyed, dimple-cheeked, musky, sweet-smelling, rhythm flowing through our fingers, sex dancing from our eyes, laughter and songs on our lips, how could we possibly be chaste? The truth was buried so deep you would have to dig straight to China to uncover it.

So there I was, thirteen years old, my tits were starting to grow, and little pubic hairs were sprouting. I was silent, and scared. I kept checking my panties, waiting for the dreaded period. My Mama's only words to me when the blood finally flowed and new eggs were released were, "Girl, make sure you don't get yourself knocked up." She gave me a box of Kotex. There were no words, no hugs, only down-eyed embarrassment. I could only think, "Mama, Mama, sweet Mama, if no one guided you with kindness and openness, how could I expect more?" Don't know, but I sure did.

As our hormones throbbed, those ugly baseball-card-playing buddies became cute. No more marbles with the boys, no, the time had come for more serious sports. The music became hotter, the dancing slower, the world more mysterious. Sex, the forbidden fruit dangling from the wicked tree of life, was unexplained and forbidden to us. Oh, what a night, oh, what a day, the flowers were in full bloom, the bees were intoxicated with nectar, and so were we.

I swear the blackboard seemed farther and farther away. The letters were too small, and I had to keep moving to the front desk 'cause I was squinting more and more each day. At this rate, I'd have early wrinkles around my eyes. I seriously needed glasses. Poverty, that heavy bag of stones, was shifting onto my shoulders. My folks could hardly make ends meet, let alone buy me glasses. Hell, when we had toothaches, they were treated with cloves until the damn things rotted down. The curse of the poor meant no dentist, and very seldom a doctor. We didn't have enough money for basic care. I dreaded the hopelessness in Mama's eyes, the sad, faraway look Daddy would get, nervously jingling his keys in his pocket when there were no answers, just sad resignation that all they could do just wasn't enough.

I needed those glasses that hot, humid summer, so I got a live-in job in some all-white beach town — Pass Christian, Mississippi. Oh, brother! It seemed so simple: I would get paid fifteen dollars a week to baby-sit and do general chores. Not so! I was stranded, living with a couple and their two bratty kids for six weeks. Plus, these kids had the nerve to always ask me why I was a nigger! The job ate up half my summer vacation, but I held my tongue, and didn't quit.

The work was easy; the two kids were petulant after I threatened that I would go home if they ever called me nigger again. They stopped, because I took good care of them, and we swam half the day on every clear afternoon. They needed me.

My problem, on the other hand, was Mr. Davis, dark-eyed, fox-eyed, wolf-tongued old fart, and a wealthy lawyer. I hated his bold looks at my newly developing body, the accidental brushings against my chest, the searing questions: "You black girls are sure pretty. Had any yet? Want some? You sure look good for a nigger girl," and on and on. Every time his wife was out of sight, he tormented me, six weeks of hell.

Irony of ironies, being pious Catholics they went to their all-white church every damn Sunday, and all the domestic workers, me included, had to go to Mass. We had to worship in the back of the church, again one of my many gripes. Like common fools we had to stand up through that long, boring service, stand up, for God's sake! I kept my mouth shut because I needed those glasses and a visit to the dentist.

Finally, mid-July I was free, driven home by the man of that wretched house and paid for six weeks of sexual harassment and servitude. But I got those glasses. The resentment stayed in my head, and my heart was weary. I was too young, too vulnerable, and just too damn smart to accept injustices like that. I was definitely not old enough to make any moves; I just kept on reading and asking obnoxious questions. Where were my answers, where were my rights?

The night hung on my shoulders, the stars shone on my soul, the gates of heaven would not open to me. The winter nights were forever cold, and the summers full of hot oppression. And time just kept on marching on, oblivious to this one little brown girl.

Chapter 8

The Rebel in Me

"Mama, there's a party at Charlotte's house this evening, can I go?" Mama looked at me with suspicion all over her face. "Whose going to chaperone you kids? Is Charlotte's mama going to be there?" Even though I lied and said yes, Mama still wouldn't let me go. She was becoming like a prison warden. My friends had gotten tired of inviting me to sleepovers and parties.

After months of agonizing and feeling trapped, I finally figured out that the way to have freedom to do all the things kids do — like going out of town, to dances, to football games, or to parties on the bay — was to be a cheerleader. Mama was so strict we could hardly cross the street without her blessing, no way, and now that we were becoming a little bit womanly, fun was out, no dates, no nothing.

I had to be a cheerleader. Yeah, my bad attitude was no help now. To be a cheerleader, you had to be voted in, be popular, liked by all, and that was not the case with me. I think I had alienated way too many kids to win any popularity contests, but no time like the present to start.

The cheerleaders' outfits were blue and white and yellow, pleated skirts down to the knees, and a modest top. I hated that outfit; the public school girls wore shorts and sleeveless tops. Oh, well, the fun of being a cheerleader outweighed the prissy uniform. Our team was always getting beat by the bigger high schools, but we tried. I began my most ambitious project ever. First I began to talk to everybody in my class. Second, I helped the poor souls who were behind in their homework. Latin, geometry, physics, you name it, for a vote, I'd come up with the work done. Lordy, Lordy, six weeks of brown-nosing, doing math problems, lending out my favorite sweater, pressing hair, covering up for my girlfriends' lies to their parents, I was shameless.

Sister Bernadette was becoming suspicious. All of a sudden, the slowest students were coming up with perfect answers, their homework done on time. I was getting nervous, too, because Sister Bernadette was about fifty years old, skinny, with beady eyes. Never laugh in her class — you'll get beat down.

She was glaring at me like she knew something. Eyes downcast, I just counted the days until the vote came in, because if I were found out, brother, I'd be in prison for life. The joys the cheerleaders had: they got to ride on the school bus and go to New Orleans, Birmingham, (Bombing ham, we called it), Montgomery, and Pensacola, Florida. I was anxious, to say the least. Plus the football players were to die for, handsome, admired, all dashing in their uniforms.

In late May the vote came up. The cheerleaders would practice through the summer to be ready for the fall season. Heaven. Both Tillie and I won, she because she was so genuinely kind and able to belt out the cheers; I won because I was the con artist who could.

You might think that cheerleading was my reward for lying and cheating — well, yes and no. All that hot, golden summer, we had so much fun rehearsing at each other's houses or in the schoolyard, "two, four, six, eight, who do we appreciate?" Nothing topped the joy of buying cloth and sewing our skirts and tops. To tell the truth, they were way too corny, but it was a Catholic school, and we had to put up with the grim rulers. The public school girls had shorts and halters, and were sexy; we weren't, but we had to live with it.

Traveling was the real reward. When October rolled around, football season began, and life opened anew. Welcome to Birmingham, Montgomery, New Orleans, Biloxi, and Pensacola. We were driving in an old yellow school bus, free as the birds, flirting our asses off with the handsomest boys with their padded shoulders, helmets, and tight pants. They didn't look at us freshmen, all shy and gawky. They had their pick of girls, so we just dreamed. Bonfires, pep rallies, parties late in the evening, meant freedom and fun.

For the first time in my life I could be out late and unaccounted for, room to fly. Tillie and I both were naïve as newborn kittens, wide-eyed, stupid, really. So when the liquor bottle was handed around, some foul-tasting homemade whisky, I had to keep up with the crowd. Tillie refused to drink, I didn't. Next thing I know I'd taken off my blouse and am running after the bus on the main highway, screaming like a drunken lunatic.

Oh, well, another hard-earned lesson: shame, scandal, disgrace, the end of freedom. Mama was so pissed off she'd look at me and glare red-hot fire. I really just felt stupid, blew the freedom ride; but the notoriety wasn't too bad — any attention beat none.

Portia, with her light brown freckled face, frizzy reddish-brown hair, and amber eyes, was one of my best friends. Tillie was another buddy, brown as walnut shells, tall, athletic, with sparkling eyes. From kindergarten's innocence — running, giggling, playing with dolls, making wishes, sharing dreams — right to high school, we were tight, these were my tree-climbing pals. We played baseball, swam at the public pool, learned to embroider pillowcases, discovered boys, had our first periods, and shared family problems. We slept over at each other's houses, and shared love. Friendship, the bridge over troubled waters; laughter, singing, crying, we shared it all. Charlotte was chubby, coffee brown, and a natural prankster. She had a houseful of brothers and sisters, and I loved them all, especially her big brother Leroy. We girls were all mad about him, but that was a joke; he was a senior and we were just lowly freshmen.

Our house was a hotbed of passion: Mama and Daddy fighting on the bad days, money short, always the threat of the lights being shut off, or the water, or the rent due — you name it, I claim it. My house was definitely not my favorite place to hang out, not at all. How I wanted normal. Portia's was my house of choice. I wished her family would adopt me; my secret desire was to live with them.

Portia's daddy was a longshoreman, tall and friendly, and her mama was full of smiles, always joked with us. They had two grandmas and two grandpas, where I felt my family had so many broken links. We only had Grandma Emma and doubts about our past because it was never discussed. It was so important to a young heart, parents who didn't fight so much, more laughter from Mama, but there were undercurrents in our house I couldn't understand.

Everybody's looking for a hero; we don't see it in ourselves. Everybody's got somebody's poster or some slogan on the wall. Nobody wants to be a hero. Nobody wants to stand tall. Medgar Wiley Evers was born near Decatur, Mississippi, July 2, 1925. I was elated to read about him in *Ebony* and *Jet* magazines! At a time when so few were vocal, this handsome, bright, college grad, army-serving man was establishing a local NAACP office in Mississippi, that state of darkness.

I loved Medgar's words: "It may sound funny, but I love the South. I don't choose to live anywhere else. There's land here where a man can raise cattle, and I'm going to do it someday. There are lakes where a man can sink a hook and fight the bass. There is room here for my children to play and grow and become good citizens, if the white man will let them."

Medgar was busy organizing boycotts of gas stations that didn't allow us to use bathrooms. He was continually in the forefront, pushing new ideas, putting his life on the line for us, constantly working against segregation laws in schools and hospitals, working to enroll voters — yep, he was busy, nonviolent, and a dreamer, a real-live hero emerging. Nobody wants to be a hero; it's so much safer on the shelf. Of course, this beautiful black man, who constantly urged that nonviolence was the only way, would eventually pay for his beliefs with his life.

The sky felt heavy that humid June afternoon. It was getting on to late, the heavens were agitated, and the fallen angels were gleeful. The immortal light of wisdom and bliss was waiting to bring Medgar home; his work in these fields was done. He was killed by an assassin's bullet, but his memory lives on, another prophet, another brother who gave his life to save ours.

We never had the tuition paid on time to those paragons of virtue, those pale ladies who, I swear, had no bodily smell. I know because my favorite thing to do was to get up close to ladies and smell them. All the black ladies smelled so sweet, and the few white ladies I was ever close to smelled good. Anyway, the nuns were constantly reminding us of our debt, loud enough for other kids to hear. Horror of horrors, the nuns gave out bags of used clothes to the less fortunate, me included in the lot. We were given these things before class was let out. In the name of their blessed Virgin, did they have no feelings? Were we really heathen savages they were sent to save? I always wondered why they lived in our neighborhood, like captives, never venturing out alone.

I swear if it wasn't for Sister Mary Margaret and Sister Theresa, there would be no hope. Sister Theresa was the younger of the two. She was beautiful all over. The tent-like white habit was concealing, but you could still see the shape of her slender, young-girl body. Her black hair had a mind of it's own, always escaping, like it was too curly to stay put. Her eyes were dark, and her mouth looked like she had lipstick on. She was most always smiling, or singing, either alone or in harmony with us girls. Believe me, this was not standard nun behavior, and we loved her.

Sister Theresa was a friend to us. We'd tease her about her legs being hidden, and she'd pull up her long skirt and dance around, lovely legs all curvy like a chorus girl, but in dumpy old-lady white cotton stockings, poor her. She loved to roll up her sleeves and show off her muscular arms. She was another mystery to us, like Sister Mary Margaret. Hard to understand how they couldn't swim, go to movie theaters, or even marry one day and have husbands and children.

We loved Sister Theresa; like Sister Mary Margaret she understood our plight. She gave me a copy of Marcus Garvey's life history. Another leader, born in Jamaica in 1919, he immigrated to America and became a profound leader, constantly preaching the need for us to migrate back to Africa. He had a huge following; in an age when the average one of us couldn't read, he gave us a voice and was leading us onward.

Mr. Garvey was eventually deported back to Jamaica for some tax-evasion charge. Sister Theresa said it was a good ploy, any reason to get rid of a powerful black voice demanding equality. Mr. Garvey believed in the purity of unmixed races, and he believed that we as mixed-race children were tainted.

I tried to accept only the greatness of him wanting equal rights. In my heart of hearts, I hated his blatant racism, especially after reading

Ida B. Wells and Frederick Douglas, who both preached racial equality. Their ideas were more to my liking. Too many good, noble white people were in agreement with us. This was not the time for racial hatred from us. Mr. Garvey indeed looked like a great African leader with his round black face, dark-as-panther eyes, and his full mouth speaking volumes in defense of our plight. His uniform looked magnificent, as did his big plumed hat. He was indeed a voice ahead of his time.

The more I complained to Mama about school, the more she'd get mad and insist we were sent to Catholic school to better ourselves. The Latin, the French, the calculus, the algebra, the chemistry — all these classes were to elevate our minds, improve our chances for success. The love of reading led me to the colored library. Beyond the narrow confines of my schoolbooks, I ventured to unknown lands.

Our own history was buried, pushed to the back of the shelf. Sojourner Truth, James Baldwin, Fredrick Douglas, George Washington Carver, Medgar Evers, Zora Neale Hurston, Gwendolyn Brooks, and Langston Hughes all stressed civil rights — better yet, demanded equality. We needed books that celebrate mother Africa, our thick lips, our coarse hair, our nostrils, our feet, and our languages. Our religions, our cultures, were so brutally destroyed. These facts were so blatantly ignored in our mis-education.

Only later did I learn how the early murderers, Christopher Columbus and his like, conquered — first the gun, then the cross. That's right, how did Africans become Christians? The cross and the gun made our own beliefs invalid. What better way to keep us in line? The white man said we black people descended from the apes, and our brains were not as developed as the Europeans'. This thinking made it easier for them to brutalize us. We were enslaved, and what we held beautiful was made ugly. The rest is history.

Glory, glory hallelujah, we will work in your blazing fields, watch you take our babies from our breast, and sell them while we nurse your own. Yeah, only religion kept us alive — what irony, saved by the cross. Go figure. Always singing, "swing low sweet chariot, coming for to carry me home." Hell, home was right here, and why did we have to die to be happy, when the rich were already happy? These questions

I asked in class were not tolerated; again I was sent home in disgrace.

I devoured the start of the NAACP. These truths fueled the fire of my soul, and I wanted more and more truth about my people. Civil rights organizations gave us a new feeling of empowerment. At last we as a people were being united.

I want to go to the church of my ancestors, black, painted bodies, drums, jungles, bush, fires, wild animals, primitive, a direct link, open communication with our Gods and our ancestors. I don't want your white life. I want the right to know and love my own. The rebel in me was developing.

August has arrived in her fiery, golden-sun glory. She brings big storms, hurricane warnings, hot, humid days, and sweaty nights. The fan is futile against the midnight heat, and we lie there sweating. The garden is overflowing with tomatoes, okra, and sunflowers, their golden heads waving, turning to face the sun. There are bushels of beans to snap, and tomatoes and cucumbers to can — work, work, work. Our kitchen boils in the heat, as rows of pickles, tomato sauces, apples, peaches, and berries are canned and properly labeled.

Like a slave I work, baby-sitting, cleaning, all with a smile, because for the first time I am traveling to Memphis alone. Betty and Peggy have the mumps, poor girls. Rags tied like scarves around their heads, their necks all swollen, sad them, lucky me. Memphis has wide tree-lined streets and a great public pool with the most handsome boys as lifeguards. Many a time we would pretend not to be able to swim, anything to get their attention. We wore swim caps to protect our pressed hair, keeping it dry so it wouldn't get nappy.

Our bathing suits were as tight and skimpy as we could get away with. We'd flirt, coyly asking for help with our backstrokes, diving, anything for attention. Memphis was sophisticated, not sprawled roads like Mobile. There were big fine cars, grand women, clubs with music drifting like sweet fog through the lit-up streets, and new kids to meet. I was elated. I was traveling alone, and Aunt Hattie and Uncle T.C. were all mine, selfish but true.

It took Grandma and Daddy to finally convince Mama to let me go. Mama was sure I'd get into trouble on the bus. Oh, please, I got into enough scrapes at home; maybe that's why she wasn't sure, can't say I blame her. Seems like after hours of instructions she decided to open the prison gate and let me go. Mama warned me, with her steely glance, "Cat, do not talk to anyone, just sit quiet."

I ignored this advice, blabbermouth that I am, like I had never heard it. In her heart of hearts, Mama knew I couldn't sit still all those hours without talking my heart out — that just was not me. There were no strangers in my world. It didn't take a brain surgeon to figure people out. Their eyes gave them away. To me, eyes were windows that told of feelings, of songs, of hurts, and joys — yep, I was just plain curious.

After quickly scanning the bus, I sat next to the good-looking young guy sitting alone. His eyes were dark and joyful. He smiled at me, and the world was mine. We were sitting in the back of the Greyhound, that glamorous chariot of the poor. He was brown as pecans, tall, full of mouth, and looked newly made. I was enchanted. David was his name, a student from New York. He was visiting his relatives in Mobile, and was just not used to this blatant segregation. I was shocked and delighted. At last, I'd found a link to the outside world. David was twenty years old and worldly. He lived in the North, and had developed an attitude that could get him killed in the South. It was a serious thing.

We got to talking, and it made the ride gentle, the day bright with new ideas, especially for me, young and eager to discover life. I would have gladly run away with him that day, ridden off into the unknown. As the day ran its course, and the night took over, I asked him shyly, "What religion do you follow? What church do you belong to? Did you ever wonder about our own ancient religions?" He looked at me so tenderly, the sky was becoming all purples and dark blues right before the blackness sets in, and his face was shadowed.

"Cat" he said, "I see Jesus in Mahatma Gandhi they left bleeding. I see him in a black brother they left hanging. Or maybe I see Jesus in you and me." His answer made me uneasy, but I felt such deep love for him — he was searching for the truth, and so was I.

Something in the way he held his head so high, something in the shadows on his face, tenderness showed through him, and I had to turn my face away. I want to go with him up into the stars, want to weep for joy, and I want to love him.

I told him my young thoughts on church and myself, how I didn't believe much that I read, felt cheated by my education. I just opened my heart, and let the words flow like some kind of soft rain; not sad, just knowing he was there to listen soothed my heart. He smiled at me so gently, and told me not to worry. "Cat, with a mind like yours, things will be revealed, just keep on questioning." Why do religions bring divisions, when they say man has risen from the beast to the God in himself? I see wars over religions, endless fires, burnings, and killings.

I swear that bus arrived in Memphis way too fast. We said goodbye in the midnight bus station, air all humid and stale, downtown streets dark and hostile. I gave David my address, and made him promise to write me. After all, he was a young brother on the road, and I loved him. I loved his deep voice, his lashes that shadowed his eyes, his slender brown hands, his face that promised good tomorrows, and his faith in me. I was happy to see aunt Hattie and Uncle T.C., but my heart rode away with a dream.

Emmett Till was born in 1941, the same year as me. He was quite a good-looking young fellow, with a cheerful smile. He was well raised by his mama, Mamie Till. He was on his yearly visit to his family's home in Mississippi. Fresh from Chicago he arrived, dapper brown young man, twinkle in his eye, merriment on his lips. At fourteen years old he was savagely beaten to death, and his body thrown into the brown Tallahatchie River. He was a sacrificial lamb. Fresh from the North, he had the nerve to wolf whistle at a young white girl. The verdict was death.

Emmet's mama cried as they fished around until they found his body, brutally tied with barbed wire, a weight around his neck. Well, those old Klan boys had big smiles on their faces as they stood around that brokenhearted scene. The law of the South was never to be questioned — "Shut up, nigger, if you want to continue to breathe."

Two black cotton pickers witnessed the abduction, and, risking their lives, went to court and accused these men of murder. The mostly white courtroom was stifling hot, the overhead fans just generally swirling their bad breezes down on them. Yes, the Klansmen laughed and smirked in court, 'cause they knew this was Mississippi, and niggers had no rights, so those murderers were acquitted. What a shame on the living!

Well, they didn't reckon on Mamie Till, her heart so broken you could see the darkness of the night, the darkness of the river bottom, as her tears were streaming. Her only son was killed. We all wept with her. His body was so crushed, his head so swollen, that he was unrecognizable, but a mama knows. He had on his daddy's ring. Well, Mamie Till took her son back to Chicago, and damn if she didn't have an open-coffin funereal so everybody could see the work of the dark side. There you have the spark of the civil rights movement. My soul quaked; my dreams, my fourteen-year-old dreams, were shattered — that could have been any one of us.

Chapter 9

Love Must Be the Answer

Seems one of my main goals in life was to be popular, but with the big mouth the Creator gave me, I was doomed to failure. Smart-ass remarks flowed from my mouth, and fights followed — hair pulling, scratching, crying, cursing, rolling on the ground, embarrassed, angry, that was me. The harder I tried to control the demons in me the more fights I got into, until one day I got it. I figured to shut my mouth and stand back. I was tired of my bad reputation, and generally tired of getting beat or beating somebody. Finally, I decided to really get to know my enemies, and win them over to my side.

Behold Eunice, one girl who always tormented me, always got my goat. I stopped fighting with her, just walked away. I decided to get to know her, since obviously she was a lot like me. One warm Saturday morning, when the winds were gentle and soft, and the sun sort of like golden butter, I went to her poor little house. This is quite a statement, because we were poor, too. I understood Eunice's anger. They were living day to day; her daddy had left, and only her tired mama was there to raise and protect them.

Miss Lou was her mama's name. She was butternut brown, with short pressed hair sticking out from the tam she always wore. Miss Lou told me that when she was young, their house had so many rotten boards she could see through the walls, and the cold always stung them. From her way of looking at things, we didn't really have it so bad. How I loved her. I could see her in Africa, a grand queen in a long indigo blue dress, her hair all nappy, and wrapped with a soft head wrap, her feet graceful on the soft green grass as her brown eyes surveyed her kingdom.

There were enough kids in that run-down old shack. I could tell Eunice was embarrassed to let me come in to visit, so we sat in the sun. My heart melted. I could see her sadness, feel her frustration. She was so beautiful, taller than all of us, and could outrun most boys. She had chocolate skin, dark, liquid eyes, long legs — she was just plain beautiful. Eunice was so happy I visited her home. I found a way to love, to step back, and cultivate a friend. At this point the politician in me was born. Kill them with kindness became my motto, popularity my goal.

What kind of religion was this that threatened us? Heaven or hell? Every Saturday night my grandma was gambling and sinning, and my daddy didn't go to church — were they dammed, too? Was Christianity the slave master's final way to straighten us out? We were multiplying way too fast. The slave foods — corn, beans, ham hocks, chicken backs, and collard greens — were making us stronger and leaner than our masters. Lord, Lord, Lord, and then the irony of Joe Louis, that nigger, beating a white man — watch out!

Joseph Louis Barrow, born in Lafayette, Alabama, was poor as the rest of the Southern blacks. With his willpower, he was determined to break the cycle of poverty, and boxing was his way out. The Brown Bomber, in 1934, knocked out James Braddock in the eighth round, and became the world champion. He retained his title longer than any other man in history. One up for us — we needed any encouragement we could get. I remember the men in our living room, listening to the Joe Louis match, and when he won, the joy was felt through the nation. He made it, and we will make it!

We hated the night Miss Dora and her husband, Mr. Rogers, came to say goodbye to us. He was taking Tillie and Kali, our longtime buddies, away from us, and we all wept. Unbelievable, they were leaving, and the feeling was sad and lonely. Mr. Rogers was urging Daddy to take us to Detroit, where every man was equal, and the pay was fair for all. Daddy said, "No, I'd just as soon stay here in Alabama." My sisters and I were mad enough to cuss pure bad words, but any argument was unheard of, so our fate was decided for us. We were doomed to segregated schools, segregated movies, and second-rate jobs.

Bobby, Tillie, Kali, Betty, and I were sitting on the front porch, devastated. The evening was coming, and the night wind was starting to blow cold. Kali sat there, staring straight ahead. His eyes were just flat, no emotion showed, which was so unusual for him. Tillie hugged and reassured me. "Don't worry, Cat, we will write y'all every week, and when you get older, you can come and visit us. Detroit isn't that far away." Bobby was silent and solemn looking. We all loved Kali and Tillie; they were like our sister and brother.

Bobby told Tillie, "We'll stay in touch, and won't ever forget y'all." At this point, Betty, Tillie, and I started crying. Serious tears rolled down our faces. I wanted to leave, too. Part of me knew I was crying because I was jealous. I wanted to leave, I wanted Daddy to pack up everything and take us all away, Grandma included. I hated losing friends. They take a piece of you, and when they leave that part of you is gone forever. The night came on, and Miss Dora and her family left. Bobby gave me one of his awkward hugs, and whispered in my ear, "Cat, you have Charlotte, Portia, Betty Ann, Corrina, and lots of friends, just relax." It seemed easy for him to say. The wind called to me, and the new moon hung above, making me confident that my world was secure.

I was fifteen, and womanhood loomed ahead. I had a little waist, a big mouth, and a bad attitude. My tits were getting way too big, so my favorite way of walking was with my head bent, eyes down, and my arms crossed over my chest. Talk about shy! Boys were becoming important. We were never told enough about sex, only that before marriage it was forbidden, and that pregnancy was the outcome. Talk about deterrents! Slow dancing, French kissing, the warm Southern skies above, and fragrant garden nights, instilled the stirrings of life. The will to couple, earth's longing, youth's yearning, that was me.

Tyrone's arms were young, and reminded me of mountains and new trees. Holding him in the sweet breeze, it felt good to be alive. There I stood in that enchanted land, my heart in my hands, the sun on my shoulders like liquid gold. Funny how the day seemed brighter when he was around, made me feel secure, my feet on the ground, head in the clouds — love, sweet, tender first love.

Naturally I was ready for love. Tyrone Bates was tall and slender, had a broad African nose and the fullest of lips. Dark as night, eyes dark and soft, his hands were gentle, and he sang all the time. He smiled like the shy guy he was. Tyrone was seventeen and divine. He drove a raggedy old car, and worked after school and on Saturdays. Of course I was forbidden to see him, but I did anyway. We'd meet in the movie theater, neck in the dark at school parties. Love come on in — I'm fifteen and alive!

Our romance didn't last long. Tyrone was older, and knew lots of girls who went all the way. I, living under my parents Nazi rules, was terrified of the actual sex part. Kissing forever, yes, rubbing, yes, sitting on laps, yes, penetration, no. As the leaves are dropped from trees, petals from spent blooms, I was discarded for the girl who gave out. This was my first encounter, but definitely not my last. Oh, no, as the song goes, "Heavenly shades of night are falling, it's twilight time." The music played sweetly on the radio and our hormones continued to multiply.

December 1, 1955 was a cold day in Montgomery, Alabama, that tired, mean, old town. Rosa Parks started something that day. She didn't look so tough, she looked almost fragile; wiry glasses, pretty light brown face, young, and slightly serious, like you could tell she read and thought a lot. She really did it that gray winter day.

Back then we coloreds had to sit in the back of the bus, starting behind the back door. If it was full, we stood, hanging on to the straps, hanging on to the backs of seats when we were little, lurching and sliding. It was really hard to see white people looking so nonchalant and important, reading their papers, silently staring straight ahead, or just plain looking through us like we were shadows.

On that gray day Miss Parks was tired, long day of work behind her, looking forward to a quiet evening, good food and rest, who knows? Miss Parks was active in civil rights, and had refused to get up before, but this time she refused to give her seat to a white man and stand up. It was bad enough we had to see pregnant women not allowed to sit.

We always got up and gave them a seat; after all, we loved each other, and our eyes spoke volumes, our African blood longed for drums to beat the new rhythm.

Miss Parks must have felt the homeland, because she would not get up. Her eyeglasses in place, clothes so neat and clean, eyes fierce like a mother lion's, she wouldn't ever again be oppressed. They called in the beef-eating white thugs, Klan boys, tobacco-chewing cops. They arrested her on the spot, and took that sweet-faced lady, white gloved, hair done nice, hat held securely on with her hatpin, to jail. The civil rights movement exploded. An ember, just softly glowing through the years, could have been dead, but Miss Parks ignited the coals, and they burst into flame.

There I was, fifteen years old and anxious, scared of being killed if I spoke out too loud. Emmett Till was murdered when we were both fourteen, then Miss Parks rekindled the fire. To hell with being scared! A woman, a tough lady, gave me courage to question, to speak out.

After I read *Tom Sawyer* by Mark Twain, my perception changed. Were there really white kids like him? How could we know, children of the storm, born innocent, raised closed off from other children because of their color? Even the movies we went to were segregated: the white kids sat downstairs, and we were in the top balcony. There were ushers to make sure we didn't mingle. The exits and entrances were separate, so there was no chance to get acquainted.

We would all look at each and wonder, us black and white kids. There was just no chance for us all to ever meet. Sad. Some of the kids smiled at us, and their eyes held the same distress as ours. *Tom Sawyer* filled me with glimmers of hope. Could there be kind people in that world, where, pitiful but true, Jim Crow ruled?

The sun streaked crimson and orange across the fading sky, like garish lipstick. The color reminded me of the hell that year had been. I was in my sophomore year, horny, pimples, broke, and not a decent boyfriend in sight. That old moon was not shining on me, and the ancient songs were too far away and distant for me to still hear. Who could I believe in if not myself?

There I stood, unwilling to be blind, deaf to the voice inside me, voiceless to the words formed inside my chest. The Catholic school had frustrated me, and all my senses were exploding. Leslie kept on writing me letters from Chicago; she wanted me to move up there because we are sisters, and the way I am going, I've got no choice. Her letters were a glimpse of another world. They lived in a second-floor apartment, for Christ's sake, over a bookstore. How strange to me, and on a busy street, no less. Sirens, lots of cops, murderers, whores, traffic, strangers milling up and down. There were kid gangs who would beat you because you didn't belong. Yikes! Was I jumping from the devil to the deep blue sea?

My back was against the wall. Mama got mad: "Girl, you are going to be the death of me"! When I came home too late from Portia's she threw a skillet full of hot grease at me. I was living in a war zone. Mama's slaps and Daddy's threats were falling on my deaf ears. Tin trumpets, they blew, bad sounds to our tender ears, and I too young to stop them. Daddy was so frustrated; he didn't like to hit us, but Mama egged him on. "J.C., these children are out of control."

Every day brought heartbreak. I had a cigar box that I filled with money from my jobs, and I told my brothers and sisters that I was planning to move to Chicago with Aunt Minnie and Leslie. Aunt Minnie knew of my struggles, and had repeatedly asked Mama to let me come up there to finish school. Mama said no, but I knew I was leaving. I was too old to be slapped and made to always feel bad about myself.

Linda looked at me with her marble-green-brown eyes all wide and worried looking, and asked, "Are you leaving me?" My heart melted like molten lava, it poured out of control, seething and burning. Betty and Peggy sat on their bed and gazed at me with such love. Their world was dear and good and bright. The stars shone, and the moon was golden and pregnant with life. Tony was so young he barely knew I was leaving. His chubby little legs and arms were dimpled and brown, he was my little brother, and my heart was part of his heart.

I wished I could take Tony with me, get a job up north, and take care of him. I wanted to wrap his brown body, all smooth and honey-smelling, in my arms. His dark eyes were wide and bright, expecting fairies and pirates to sail over the clouds. Tony was a dreamer like me. Mama was not getting any better. She was always sick — run-down, she called it. The linoleum was cold under my bare feet, and kept me from burning up inside. Our house was a ship of hope and glory, china dishes, lace curtains, beatings, and hugs. Childhood was wasted on me.

Bobby was planning on going to the army, voluntarily; everyone approved, bravo! I, on the other hand, was pretty much a disgrace. Teachers were hostile, and I had been suspended far too many times. My heart beat strong and true. Love sat on my right side, and compassion covered my soul. I wanted to help myself, to live, help my people, help this old, sad, lost world. Chicago scared me. Leslie writes of elevated trains, gray cold winters, overcoats, and sullen stares, nothing glamorous from her mouth. She doesn't embroider her reality. She just tells it like she sees it.

I had to go; the winds were calling me. Why can't the South be home for us all? Where do I belong? Where is there a place where I can feel secure, where the color of my skin doesn't matter, or my religion? Soft green earth, red clay roads, sweet summer evenings cooling off the parched earth, nightingales, and music. Alabama was a soft country really, quiet enough to hear the nights sing. I was leaving my home with the knowledge that I would return when I was older and well lived.

Sweet sixteen, and May was hot as hell, all the bushes and trees shrouded with dust from the red clay roads. The shops were shaded, and the streets were deserted in the hot afternoons. You could hear the ball game from radios on the block. All was quiet, and the fans were running in most every house.

I wanted to leave hot, ignorant, snuff-dipping, tobacco-chewing Alabama. Hell, everybody seemed to move in slow motion to me, slow, scared, eager to not make waves. There were too many killings and beatings. Lou Ann and Maria, two girls from our school, were raped by some white boys down by the creek, and nothing was done. The law was definitely not on our side.

Martin Luther King, Medgar Evers, new leaders, countless voices were rising, and I was stuck in the quicksand of the South. My parents forbade under pain of banishment any involvement in civil rights meetings. I was so mad — my Dad used to have secret union meetings; our turn around, he said no. I guess I could understand it, he was raised in Mississippi and had seen enough killing.

My soul was on fire. While the nuns droned on and on about Shakespeare, dead black bodies were floating in our rivers. Our world was exploding, and we were expected to memorize Latin? Already I had a coffee can that I slowly filled with money for my trip north. Felt like I was outgrowing my skin. The train at night wailed in the distance, promising faraway lands, sweet streets paved with gold, and kind faces not prejudiced against you at every step. Me, the naïve dreamer, head full of hopes and visions, I was leaving.

In the hot, fragrant yard, the little song sparrow sang his lullaby, and the very air was alive with dreams being born. There seemed to be no hope for me here, let alone for Bobby. How I wish Bobby could go to college. He was bright, and not a blighter like me. He took it all too serious. He was an altar boy. He prayed and believed in miracles. Me, I believed the sun rose every morning and the new air was sweet.

Bobby should go to college — hell, at least he would be an honest businessman, the straight-as-an-arrow brother, the scholar. While I wreck the world, he picks up the pieces and tries to bring things together. The scholarships are few and far between. Bobby lost out to Alice, a girl in his class just as smart as he. Bobby decided to join the army. Mama would get an eighty-dollar monthly allotment check, and he would get money and college benefits. It is so sad to me, Bobby joining the army. Isn't that the place where Daddy said blacks get jobs unloading ammunition from boats, cook, clean, and are the first on the front line?

My brother didn't listen. I did. Lots of black girls were signing for the women's army. Not me. I wanted to be a poetess and live in Greenwich Village in New York — a dreamer, that was me. Bobby was content to follow the rules; I fought them. My big brother, from the night we escaped from Mississippi till now, the brown-eyed, Band-Aid, lemonade, kind-word brother, was leaving home, and I felt my little world shift.

Oh me, oh my, May time, school so hot, the air so still, the flies won't even buzz. The shades were half drawn in that big old room, and the world was closing in on me. Daddy traced this big increase in violence — these cross burnings, bombings, beatings, false arrests, deaths, and rapes — on the black soldiers coming home to the South, Jim Crow land.

The times were changing: these soldiers had been in Paris, Germany, Rome, and Africa. They came back home to nigger land, back of the bus, no vote, no good jobs. Lower your eyes, boys, and welcome home.

Civil rights demands were increasing, and still my schoolroom seemed to be in a time warp, a vacuum. We had no civil rights rally, no after-school organizing like the public schools did. The black Protestant churches were full-ahead on rights. There was nothing here but ancient lies. Our history was a lie, and there was nothing to uplift us.

I've had it! That white uniform was damp and gray from being washed too many times. My shoes were run-down on the sides, and my soul was weary. Unmarked graves dotted the land in rural Alabama. There were dead bodies in rivers, and Shakespeare stood tall over me.

Jeez, I must have been drunk on the nectar of life, the passion of May, that golden, lavender, pink month. I had to be drunk on life, on brown skin, on love and compassion, delirious with the pride of black men and women. I felt triumphant, my heart joyous from songs and dances, sweet smells from sweet dark dusky bosoms.

Father Albert was visiting our class that hot May day. I couldn't stand the man. He was skinny, with lean, bony fingers, a balding head, and stern eyes hidden behind thick glasses. Never — I'm talking never — would the man discuss civil rights, Martin Luther King Jr., Medgar Evers, nobody.

That day, when he began his boring end-of-the-school-year talk, I asked about Jesus and black people. "Where are the black priests and nuns to guide us? Where is my African religion? Who am I? And definitely who the hell are you to not tell me about my history, and the crimes committed in the name of Christ?" I kept talking until he told me to leave Heart of Mary forever, for to question the faith was the final sin. I went.

There I was, sixteen and leaving, after being thrown out of school for the last time. I managed to save enough money for fare to get to

Chicago. Aunt Minnie said I could live with them. Funny, when I finally had my bus ticket in hand, my little brown suitcase packed, my room cleaned out and given to Betty, I felt devastated.

That old house held my spirit, my dreams; the fears, the tears, the loud laughter were imprinted in the walls here, and for the first time I was terrified. There I was, leaving green lanes and country roads, the bay and fresh fish, for the unknown world of cement and lights.

I remember the day I left, walked on through that garden gate. The air was soft and fragrant, the willow trees swayed in the breeze, and the azaleas were dazzling in their beauty. I swear my heart was breaking, and the honeysuckles were aching in their glory. Where was I? What was I seeking? Drunk on life, I stumbled, blind, young, ignorant, and vulnerable. I begged my angel to walk with me, stand by my side because she had always been there, through the slaps, the hits, the salty tears of forgiveness, the acid rain of racism, the lash of the whip, the smell of the magnolias on the dirt road. I prayed, "Sweet angel in your lavenders and blues stand by me." I was young and had a dream to follow.

It hurt me so bad to look at my mama, her dress so neat and freshly pressed, her hair a glossy black, and her heart as broken as mine. All of a sudden the day was too bright, and Mama was streaming tears because I was leaving, and all the words left unsaid, all the scars unhealed, were piled up there behind our eyes. I, who thought I could never love again, fell down the bottomless pit of loneliness, not to mention leaving my brothers and sisters. What a day! Sixteen years old and my world was beginning and ending.

How little was I prepared for the outside world that tender day? Daddy drove me to the bus station. He made a few feeble jokes, and never once did he look at me. All his hopes were in his children, and already, I, the rebel, was leaving for the North, the unknown place of big buildings and strangers. "It gets bitter cold, and the people are not friendly," were his words of advice. He also reassured me again, "Honey, the door is always open." That freed me. I knew I could always come home again.

Felt like I never meant it to turn out this way, seems my life took a different path, and following my dreams, I strayed. The road of life got so rough, and I kept falling down, but I knew how to stand again. Where was my angel when I needed her to walk me through the sands of time? I was so young and tender, here for such a little while. The search for the truth had set me free to question, and in questioning I had become defiant and angry.

My folks knew that the South was too rough for me, and my actions would likely get a cross burned in our front yard, or our house burned. The time had come for this hardheaded girl to go north for a while. There I was riding on the back of the bus, carrying the brown bag chock-full of fried chicken, pound cake, and bananas. I was sent off with a full belly. I was all dressed to kill in my new handmade skimpy dress, my cheap slippers, and one bag full of clothes.

From bare beginnings the magic starts.

Hoy Kersh

Hoy Kersh is a songwriter and music performer living in the woods of Northern California. She has produced two albums, toured the country with reggae artists, and has MC'ed for Reggae on the River. While living in Jamaica, she built an organic farm and taught reading and writing to eight to 80-year-olds in the local night school. She is currently working with students at a rural Pacific Northwest school on a video documentary about logging and the regional water crisis. Her writing has inspired her students to positive action in local environmental issues. A lifelong antiwar activist, Hoy continues to be active in local and regional movements.